The
MORTGAGE
GAME

The
MORTGAGE
GAME

The **5** Cs
and How to
Connect Them

MANNY KAGAN

Published by Advantage, Charleston, South Carolina.
Member of Advantage Media Group.

ADVANTAGE is a registered trademark and the Advantage colophon is a trademark of Advantage Media Group, Inc.

Printed in the United States of America.

ISBN: 978-159932-323-7
LCCN: 2012949490

This publication is designed to provide accurate and authoritative information in regard to the subject matter covered. It is sold with the understanding that the publisher is not engaged in rendering legal, accounting, or other professional services. If legal advice or other expert assistance is required, the services of a competent professional person should be sought.

Advantage Media Group is proud to be a part of the Tree Neutral® program. Tree Neutral offsets the number of trees consumed in the production and printing of this book by taking proactive steps such as planting trees in direct proportion to the number of trees used to print books. To learn more about Tree Neutral, please visit www.treeneutral.com. To learn more about Advantage's commitment to being a responsible steward of the environment, please visit www.advantagefamily.com/green

Advantage Media Group is a leading publisher of business, motivation, and self-help authors. Do you have a manuscript or book idea that you would like to have considered for publication? Please visit www.advantagefamily.com or call 1.866.775.1696

I'd like to dedicate this book to my wife and partner Elfa, who has walked this life journey with me for 45 years.

Table of Contents

Introduction

Home ownership is one of the major components of the American Dream. However, to participate in this dream, most people need a mortgage. Obtaining a mortgage can be complicated, competitive, and intimidating. How does a person even get started in this process?

Is this something you want to research on your own? Wouldn't you rather trust the services of an expert and proven leader in the field? If you'd rather work with an expert, you should read this book.

Why does a person even need a mortgage? The answer to this question can be found in the brief anecdote of a drill. Suppose you need a hole in the wall for a specific purpose. Well, a drill is one way to get that hole. Similarly, a mortgage is just a financial tool for acquiring real estate.

We live in challenging times. Many people own their homes, or other pieces of real estate, and they would like to cash in on historic low rates by obtaining even more property. Simultaneously, even though millions of others have lost their homes, they still would like to start over and buy again.

Despite these challenges, the American Dream is still very much alive. Many borrowers would like to improve their cash flow by refinancing their existing mortgages, a process that will help boost the economy. Meanwhile, lenders are being forced to tighten guidelines for mortgage qualification and millions of borrowers cannot qualify. Is there a solution? Yes, if you know what lenders need and how to find it.

I have been in the mortgage business for twenty-nine years and I have seen it all. In this book, I will share many of my secrets. You will learn the answers to your mortgage questions.

When I started writing this book, I had to find a catchy title. Soon I discovered that many of the titles I liked were taken. Finally, my wife, Elfa, came up with *The Mortgage Game*. This title is a perfect fit. The process of getting a mortgage, as you will soon discover, has very specific rules—just like a game does. I call these rules the "Five Cs": collateral, capacity, credit, capital, and character. To win in the mortgage game, you need to know how to follow the rules and to have fun while playing. A friend of mine, who works for a major bank, mentioned that there should be a sixth C: common sense. Unfortunately, common sense has left the mortgage business.

This book is separated into two parts: a dry part—a description of the mortgage industry and its rules—and a fun part—my personal stories, as well as client anecdotes. I'll begin by sharing a story about how to buy a house in heaven (my adaptation of an old joke).

Before his death, the head of the mafia instructed his top three lieutenants (a hit man, an attorney, and a banker) to each put $100,000 in his coffin. After the funeral, the lieutenants gathered for a drink at their favorite restaurant. "My boss was like a father to me," said the chief hit man. "Without hesitation, I put $100,000 in his coffin. I've heard from my priest that there are angels called cherubim who are protecting heaven with their swords. Our boss will need to buy some ammunition to deal with them."

"That's all baloney," said the attorney. "The boss was like a brother to me. I put $100,000 in the coffin because the boss will need to deal with *the judge, St. Peter, to get to heaven. The gates to heaven are old and squeaky. They might benefit from some grease."*

"The boss was my best friend and a smart cookie," said the banker. "I'm sure he will find a way to get to heaven. While there, he'll need to get good accommodations. Maybe a house with a nice view. To get one of those, he will need a substantial down payment, so he can get a mortgage. Because banks do not allow cash but are okay with gifts, I wrote a gift letter. Since those guys in heaven want to be sure I have sufficient funds to support that letter, I put a check for $300,000 in the coffin and took your cash to deposit in my account."

This story shows only one of the ways to finance real-estate acquisition. Keep reading to find more.

MY STORY

I was born in 1947 in Riga, Latvia to a middle class family. At that time, Latvia was part of the former Soviet Union. My father worked as the manager of a government meat store and my mother was a teacher. I had a younger brother and sister. Even though we lived in a tiny apartment, we were a very happy family.

I was a good student, although perhaps a little bit lazy at school. In Latvia, some kids (including me) went to work at age fifteen. This was because people needed two years of work experience to get into a good college. I ended up becoming an apprentice to a tool-and-dye maker in a radio factory. Since I was small, the other workers had to put a bench beneath me so that I could reach the vise at my workstation. I learned a lot in that factory. My mentor, Uncle Vanya, had dozens of tools in his drawer, including sixteen different kinds of hammers alone. Eventually, I learned how to use all of those tools—although never as well as Uncle Vanya.

At age seventeen, I started college. My major was automation and telemechanics, a natural choice given my experience in the radio factory. Soon, I met Elfa. When I was twenty, after dating for a year, Elfa and I got married. I left my day studies, continued at night, and went back to work to support our family. I actually went back to work at the same radio factory I had worked in as a teenager. This time, I was hired as an engineer.

In 1968, our family decided to emigrate. We wanted to go to Israel. In order to get my visa, I had to leave my engineering work, since the factory had military contracts. Instead, I went to work as a car mechanic in a garage run by a family friend.

Unfortunately, at first the government declined our request to emigrate. For the next three years, we were known as *refuseniks*. This was a challenging time. Because of my refusal to become a Soviet citizen, I got expelled from college. My expulsion resulted in an automatic army draft.

Miraculously, I was saved from the draft because, while working in the garage, I had been enrolled in military driving school. Due to this enrollment, my military draft was postponed. Then, since my family was not permitted to leave the country and we refused our Soviet citizenship, the college had to reinstate me.

Meanwhile, Elfa participated in demonstrations, demanding that the government let us go. This got her arrested. Over the next three years, while we continually confronted the government, I began the project of remodeling our apartment. The scarcity of everything, including building materials, added to the challenges we faced. Finally, we were told we would never be permitted to leave Latvia. I finished the remodel on our apartment. Just one day later, an OVIR government representative who dealt with *refuseniks* paid us a visit. After seeing our remodeled apartment, the official wanted it for himself. Immediately, we received permission to leave. Three weeks later, we were on a plane flying to Israel via Vienna. This was in January 1972.

For the first six months of our time in Israel, we had to stay in an absorption center. There, we learned Hebrew and become acclimated. Eventually I was hired as an engineer, to work in a factory that produced corrugated boxes. I advanced quickly and moved on. Next, I landed at an international company that produced edible oil. There, I was the project manager in charge of company factory construction, which took place all over the world. When the company ran out of new construction projects, I had to plan for my future. I decided to begin my MBA studies at Jerusalem University. My dream, though, was to finish my MBA in the United States.

After dealing with the challenges of obtaining American visas, my family arrived in San Francisco in August 1980. My wife and I brought our two daughters and my mother-in-law, who had always lived with us. Our family of five knew only one person, an old friend of my wife's. This friend arranged for us to live, temporarily, in a hotel in the Tenderloin District. Our window looked out onto a daily parade of pimps and prostitutes in the street below. Later, we rented a small apartment. Elfa, an artist, wanted to have a career as a fashion designer; thus, she enrolled at the Louis Salinger Academy of Fashion. In the meantime, I was accepted into the MBA program at Golden Gate University.

While I was in school, I began to look for an opportunity to make a living. I took manual labor jobs and worked my way back up the ladder again. In 1982, I was hired as vice president of the Helga Howie Fashion Company, a women's high-fashion business that was losing money. Unfortunately, my lack of experience in the fashion industry did not help improve the company's finances much.

My wife and I also became involved in Amway, a multilevel company, where I met Tom Grundy, a mortgage bank sales manager. He invited me to lunch and told me all about the mortgage business. While I didn't have a clue about what the business entailed, his brief presentation interested me. I asked him how much money I could make in the industry and he offered a figure that sounded very attractive to me. The figure was double my salary at that time. He told me that if I wanted to do get into the industry, I could; after all, where there is a will there is a way. At the end of our conversation, I asked him one final question: "Where do I sign?" That's how I became a mortgage professional.

MORTGAGES 101
Exploring The Mortgage Game's Rules

Before we start, we must answer a very basic question. What is a mortgage and what does it do?

The word *mortgage* is cloaked in contradictions:

- A mortgage is not a product, nor is it a service, but it has a price.
- To create it, many trees have to be cut, but it is difficult to see the final result of that action.
- It is a thousand years old and it is reborn every day.
- It is used by millions but needs to be tailored to each individual.
- Many people would like to obtain a mortgage, but no one really wants to have one.
- A mortgage can make a person rich, but it can also make a person poor.
- It can create joy or cause disaster.
- While it does not discriminate, it is unattainable for many.
- Many people sell mortgages, but only a few know how to get them.
- Mortgages can help to stimulate the economy or bring a government to its knees.
- Politicians, who have no idea how mortgages function, are the ones who crate the laws to regulate them.

- According to the following table, the term is used in only thirty states, but it is known all over the world.

What, then, is a mortgage, exactly?

Most people who want to purchase real-estate property, and do not have enough money to pay for it outright, need a mortgage. They might have a certain percentage of the sales price they can offer for a down payment. However, for the balance of the purchase price, they need to find a lender who will give them a loan. Such a loan has specific terms and conditions attached. Once the loan is approved, the borrowers, sellers, and other parties sign and record documents; after that, borrowers receive keys to their property. Then, borrowers are required to make regular monthly payments to the lenders.

The above concept, called *paid as agreed*, is the cornerstone of the lending business. Before receiving any loan money, borrowers are required to sign a huge pile of various legal documents.

One of those documents is called a *note*. This is the most important document of them all since it describes the loan's terms and conditions. The note is accompanied by another document that outlines the property that will be used as collateral (that is, as a pledge). This document is either called a *security deed*, a *deed of trust*, or, simply, a *mortgage*. The document's name varies by state, according to each state's foreclosure laws. Regardless of the differences between state terminologies, *mortgage* has become the generic term for everything related to property lending. You can see which states use the term *mortgage* as a security instrument in the following chart:

Mortgage or Deed of Trust by State

Abbreviations	State	Security Instrument	Abbreviations	State	Security Instrument
AL	Alabama	Mortgage	MT	Montana	Deed of Trust
AK	Alaska	Deed of Trust	NE	Nebraska	Deed of Trust
AZ	Arizona	Deed of Trust	NV	Nevada	Deed of Trust
AR	Arkansas	Mortgage	NH	New Hampshire	Mortgage
CA	California	Deed of Trust	NJ	New Jersey	Mortgage
CO	Colorado	Deed of Trust	NM	New Mexico	Deed of Trust
CT	Connecticut	Mortgage Deed	NY	New York	Mortgage
DE	Delaware	Mortgage	NC	North Carolina	Deed of Trust
DC	District of Columbia	Deed of Trust	ND	North Dakota	Mortgage
FL	Florida	Mortgage	OH	Ohio	Mortgage
GA	Georgia	Security Deed	OK	Oklahoma	Mortgage
HI	Hawaii	Mortgage	OR	Oregon	Deed of Trust
ID	Idaho	Deed of Trust	PA	Pennsylvania	Mortgage
IL	Illinois	Mortgage	RI	Rhode Island	Mortgage
IN	Indiana	Mortgage	SC	South Carolina	Mortgage
IA	Iowa	Mortgage	SD	South Dakota	Mortgage
KS	Kansas	Mortgage	TN	Tennessee	Deed of Trust
KY	Kentucky	Mortgage	TX	Texas	Deed of Trust
LA	Louisiana	Mortgage	UT	Utah	Deed of Trust
ME	Maine	Mortgage	VT	Vermont	Mortgage
MD	Maryland	Deed of Trust	VA	Virginia	Deed of Trust
MA	Massachusetts	Mortgage	VI	Virgin Islands	Mortgage
MI	Michigan	Mortgage	WA	Washington	Deed of Trust
MN	Minnesota	Mortgage	WV	West Virginia	Deed of Trust
MS	Mississippi	Deed of Trust	WI	Wisconsin	Mortgage
MO	Missouri	Deed of Trust	WY	Wyoming	Mortgage

Source: Document Systems, Inc.

I found a provocative definition of the word *mortgage* in an article by Gareth Maples: "The history of the word is very interesting. *Mort* is from the Latin word for death and *gage* means a pledge to forfeit something of value if a debt is not repaid." In other words, *mortgage* is literally a death pledge. It is "dead" for two reasons: first, the property is forfeited or "dead" to the borrower if the loan isn't repaid; second, the pledge itself is "dead," or terminated, if the loan is repaid.

Maples' article explains that mortgages were mentioned in England as early as 1190. Eventually, settlers brought the concept to the Americas in the early 1900s. When Franklin D. Roosevelt became president of the United States, he had the idea of creating a consumer-friendly nation. As a result, the Federal Housing Administration (FHA) was created in 1934. The FHA ensured mortgage lenders against losses from default. When risk was taken away from the lenders, they were more willing to lend money. The FHA developed the thirty-year, fixed-loan program. In order to make the FHA function better, in 1938 the government established the Federal National Mortgage Association, or Fannie Mae, which bought FHA-insured loans and sold them on the securities market.

That system worked fine for decades. In the 1970s, when the Baby Boomers entered the workplace, the government created another organization to support mortgages: the Federal Home Loan Mortgage Corporation, or Freddie Mac. Through Freddie Mac, the government was able to increase the supply of mortgage funds available to commercial banks, savings and loan institutions, credit unions, and other mortgage lenders. This way, the government could control the flow of money, which made funds more available for Americans.

Today, the government owns Fannie Mae and Freddie Mac, both of which are practically bankrupt. If the government did not support them, the whole system would collapse. As long as those organizations exist and offer relatively low interest rates, there is no way for Wall Street or private parties to develop other competing organizations, as they did in the past.

WHAT ARE MORTGAGES' SOURCES?

Before we can fully understand how these loan organizations work, we have to answer another simple question: where does the money for these loans come from? As we know, to obtain a mortgage, borrowers have to go to a bank. As we also know, banks already have our money. Therefore, the process goes through the following steps. First, the government prints money. When we are paid for our labor, we receive that money. We deposit money into banks, earning little or no interest. Then, the banks turn around and lend this money, our collective money, to anyone who needs a loan, which has become known as a mortgage. Banks charge higher interest rates for these loans than they pay people for the privilege of safeguarding this money, and that difference is known as the *margin of profit.*

Banks have profited greatly from the margin-of-profit formula because they can also borrow money from the government at very low interest rates. (At the start of 2012, for example, that rate was a quarter of 1 percent.) All of this worked well until banks became greedy and got involved in practices that went against the mortgage industry's very foundation.

Let's look at the broader picture. In the United States, there are different types of banks. We used to have savings-and-loans banks, which were viable options for those wanting a safe place in which they could deposit and save their money. After a number of crashes in recent years, the savings-and-loan industry disappeared. Big banks swallowed the smaller banks. Today, as a result, there are basically five major banks that control the flow of money in the United States.

In recent years, credit unions have become an important part of the cash-flow system, but they are regulated by different organizations and rules. Though these credit unions offer mortgages, the majority of borrowers still choose to go to a bank, simply because most banks have a widespread branch system.

In the past, banks had limited funds and limited geographic concentration; they could not afford to lower interest rates. The government evaluated this scenario and stepped in after deciding that the country needed to have a period of growth (that is, the government wanted to provide an opportunity to increase home ownership). The government believed this was a good political decision that could stimulate the economy.

To put this theory in motion, Washington gave the green light to Wall Street, encouraging the creation of tools that would circulate housing money. Since Fannie Mae and Freddie Mac were practically owned by the government, Washington could print money for them; yet, at the same time, the two companies were publicly traded on Wall Street. This combination allowed money to be circulated all over the country. It did not matter where loans originated. They all ended up connected to Fannie Mae, Freddie Mac, or other Wall Street investors.

In turn, this allowed the creation of universal underwriting guidelines that changed the way banks could do business. This set of guidelines (and restrictions) became known as the Fannie Mae and Freddie Mac Underwriting Guidance. The flow of money through Wall Street helped breed mortgage banks. These new companies could originate loans, package them, and sell them to investors on Wall Street through a secondary market, right alongside Fannie Mae and Freddie Mac. Unlike typical banks, mortgage banks do not have depositors; their money comes from lines of credit. To sell their products, mortgage banks need an outside sales force. Determining how to fill this need is how the mortgage brokerage industry was created. Mortgage brokers became sales representatives who did not work for mortgage banks; instead, they peddled the banks' products.

Meanwhile, the large pools of money involved in this system allowed Wall Street firms to create new loan programs with new underwriting guidelines, different from those of Fannie Mae and Freddie Mac. In turn, these new programs and guidelines created competition. The big players used different, innovative devices that increased the risk of the mortgages. For example, a company could increase a loan's loan-to-value ratio (LTV), essentially eliminating the loan's security. Before these new guidelines were developed, potential borrowers had to prove they had adequate income and thus an ability to pay back the loan. All at once, this concept went out the window. Suddenly, anyone could qualify for a loan, regardless of income or assets. The writing was on the wall. If anyone could get a loan—and everyone who believed in the American Dream wanted to have a mortgage, sooner or later—investors would not be able to sustain the lending burden. In fact, they couldn't, which is why the industry collapsed in 2008.

Today, the federal government has total control of what is happening in the mortgage industry. It owns Fannie Mae and Freddie Mac outright. It also has control over FHA (Federal Leasing Authority) and VA (Veteran's Administration) loans. The mortgage industry has become a cash mechanism for the government. We have low interest rates in 2012, an election year, because the federal government decided to keep them low, which is done by printing more money.

Recently, the government decided it needed to cut taxes. To allow this, lawmakers in the House of Representatives passed HP3630, which allows the government to increase fees charged in mortgage transactions. Those people who borrow money from Fannie Mae and

Freddie Mac today will end up paying higher costs or even higher interest rates at the expense of lowering federal taxes for the rest of the population. On one hand, the government gives; on the other, the government takes.

The federal government created or allowed the rules and laws that brought Wall Street to its knees. These legal changes were an attempt to stimulate the economy, and they failed miserably. Now, after the crash and all of its related fallout, the government continues to keep interest rates low. Still, many people are not qualified to refinance or to buy new properties. In other words, the system is still out of balance.

Later in this book, we'll examine mortgage banks, mortgage brokers, mortgage-backed securities, and reverse mortgages. We'll also examine a new type of transaction, underwater mortgages, in which the value of the mortgage is higher than the value of the home. The mortgage business is a billion-dollar industry and the federal government controls 70 percent of it.

MORTGAGES AS A COMMODITY

When a consumer obtains a mortgage, a bank gives him or her the money either from its deposits—account holders' collective money— or through a line of credit. When granting a deposit-based loan, or a *portfolio loan*, a bank can be more flexible in its underwriting rules. When a loan is granted through a line of credit, the lender's intention is to sell the loan in a secondary market; in that case, the purchaser of the loan provides guidelines for the loan source and the underwriting. Fannie Mae and Freddie Mac—or, in the past, other investors— have packaged huge numbers of loans together.

How did this work? Through packaging, investors could create mortgage-backed securities. These mortgage-backed securities would then be sold as mortgage bonds to the federal government, foreign governments, holders of large pension plans, and individuals who wanted to buy secure investments. Mortgage-backed securities became an alternative investment tool for people who wanted to diversify their portfolios.

As a result of this packaging, interest rates would fluctuate according to the economy's fluctuation. If investors felt they could make more money by investing in corporate stocks, they would pull money from bonds and buy stocks, which would immediately raise the mortgage interest rate. If, in contrast, they felt the stock market was not doing well, they would pull money from their stocks and place it in mortgage bonds. This practice would lower the interest rate. Today, there are no fluctuations like this because the government controls the interest rate. However, changes in the world market can affect the interest rate at any time.

TOOLS OF THE TRADE

When a borrower applies for a loan, his personal circumstances determine what kind of loan he can get, based on all of the Five Cs. Major and commercial banks have two choices for handling these loans: they can keep the loans themselves—in other words, they can charge an interest rate based on their own underwriting guidelines—or they can sell the loans in a secondary market.

FIXED-RATE LOANS

As we learned in the previous chapter, loans sold in a secondary market—usually to Fannie Mae and Freddie Mac—are bound to specific interest rates that are set daily and tied to Wall Street's fluctuation. Those loans have a fixed interest rate and are called *fixed-rate loans*. In other words, the rate will never change during the life of the loan. A fixed-interest loan could last ten, fifteen, twenty, twenty-five, thirty, or even forty years. This type of loan must be paid in equal installments, the amounts of which are determined through a process called *amortization*. A loan is amortized at different rates, depending on the loan's length. In general, the longer the loan's duration, the higher its interest rate and the lower its monthly payments will be. In cases of shorter loans, payments will be higher because those loans have to be repaid more quickly.

Fixed-rate loans (also called *fully amortized loans*) are made up of two components: first, they include a principal amount that needs to be repaid; second, they include interest, which is money a borrower pays above and beyond the principal for the privilege of receiving the loan in the first place. The faster a borrower pays down the principal, the less the amount of interest. Paying down a loan quickly also has an opposite effect on tax deduction, one of the major benefits of possessing a mortgage. Year after year, as the loan is repaid, the amount of tax deduction a borrower can claim goes down.

My clients Jerry and Jane wanted to buy their first home. They fell in love with a small house and thought they could bid around $800,000. After their low-ball offers were rejected numerous times, they were ready to go for a higher price. Their next offer was $900,000.

When my company started working on their loan, the fixed-rate loan limit was $729,000. By the time we were ready to move forward, Fannie Mae's limits had gone down to $625,000. Jerry and Jane's loan amount was $720,000, and the thirty-year fixed rate was 4.75 percent. Jerry thought this percentage was too high, but Jane was adamant about obtaining a fixed-rate loan. So, we found another solution: we would divide the mortgage into two loans. The first was a fixed-rate loan of $625,000 over thirty years. This loan had an interest rate of 4.125 percent. The remaining balance of $95,000, which would be placed on an equity line of credit, had an adjustable rate tied to the prime rate at 3.25 percent plus the margin. The equity-line payments were interest-only payments, which could have solved the problem.

As it turned out, there was another option: Jerry and Jane could take out a fixed-rate loan for $720,000 for only ten years. This was their final decision.

PORTFOLIO LOANS

Portfolio loans are regulated by different rules and guidelines; therefore, they have much more flexibility. Portfolio loans allow those people who cannot qualify for Fannie Mae and Freddie Mac loans to obtain new mortgages. Those loans are often adjustable-rate mortgages (ARMs), which have a fixed three-, five-, or ten-year period.

ADJUSTABLE LOANS

A borrower who does not qualify for a fixed-rate loan often chooses to accept a portfolio loan. Many times, that loan comes in the form of what's called an *adjustable loan*. Adjustable loans fall into several different categories, and in every case interest rates fluctuate. They can change once a month, every six months, or once a year. Today, many adjustable loans are fixed for longer periods of time. Common time frames include three, five, seven, or ten years.

Even though those payback periods are longer, the loans are still referred to as "adjustable." That's because after that fixed period of time—say, three years—the loan's interest rate will adjust according to the index to which the loan was attached at the outset, plus a fixed margin. In such a case, the borrower can either agree to the new interest rate, choose to pay off the loan's remaining balance, or refinance at one of the various rates currently available.

Adjustable loans have caps on both the low and high ends, but some borrowers are still intimidated by them because their interest rates can increase after a fixed period of time. It is common, however, for borrowers to refinance at a lower rate when the loans mature. Today, for example, borrowers who took loans seven years ago are benefiting from much lower rates in both adjustable and fixed-interest loans. Currently, as market indices such as Libor, the 11th District Cost of Funds, and the T-Bill remain low, adjustable loans have lower rates (as low as 3 percent) compared to low fixed rates.

Another type of loan allows a borrower to pay only the interest and none of the principal amount. This is called an *IO*, or an *interest-only loan*. An IO works when a loan is fixed for a period of time— let's say for five years. During this time, payment is based only on interest. There is no amortization for this type of loan because the lender does not expect the principal amount to be paid back, *per se*. These loans usually have a slightly higher interest rate and lower payments than amortized loans do. In the past, when real estate's appreciation was guaranteed, an interest-only loan sometimes ended up saving the borrower money. In contrast, today, when real-estate value can plummet, as we have so clearly seen, an interest-only loan can be a risky proposition.

GOVERNMENT LOANS

In spite of the fact that the federal government controls most of the mortgages granted in the United States, lenders still use the term *government loans* for three categories of loans: FHA, VA, and USDA loans. Regardless of which government agency is involved, conventional banks finance all government loans.

The FHA was created in 1934. Its main mission was to insure banks' losses caused by mortgages. Before 1934, banks would lend money for only five years. They would extend a loan only if a borrower could provide a significant percentage of the purchase price as a down payment. To create affordability and lower monthly payments, the FHA introduced a thirty-year, fixed-rate program and required a much smaller down payment. These types of loans, known as *FHA loans*, became hugely popular and served as an economic stimulus. Taking such a loan was a new way to buy into the American Dream.

Until a few years ago, limits for FHA loans stayed low and were not popular in big cities such as San Francisco, where I do most of my business. Now, ever since agency jumbo limits were lowered, FHA programs have the highest loan limits around. The FHA has kept the limit at $729,750, depending on the geographic area, and at $1,403,400 for four units.

When limits increased, matching Fannie Mae and Freddie Mac's limits, the balance shifted. Now, if a borrower is amenable to purchasing mortgage insurance, he can obtain an FHA loan with as little as 3.5 percent down and a credit score as low as 560.

Mortgage insurance, of course, is an extra cost. While it is associated with FHA loans, it is also an option for those seeking a conventional loan with only 5 percent down. Because of their higher lending limits and more underwriting flexibility, FHA loans are very popular. Currently, the government is considering using FHA loans as a solution for refinancing loans that were not sold to Fannie Mae and Freddie Mac and that exceed current property value.

The second type of government loan is a *VA loan*. In 1944, the government created the VA to help veterans of World War II. Among other things, the VA offered a guarantee on loans for eligible military veterans and National Guard members. While this type of loan did not require any down payment, it did require an upfront fee that was included in the loan's balance. Today, limits on VA loans are similar to those on conventional loans for a single-family house. The procedure for calculating loan limits for 2012 has changed. At present, the VA doesn't impose a maximum amount an eligible veteran may borrow using a VA-guaranteed loan. Instead, loan limits establish the maximum possible guarantee for a loan. This maximum varies from $417,000 to $625,000, depending on the geographic area. The best way to find information on VA loan eligibility and loan limits is through the VA website, http://www.benefits.va.gov/homeloans/eligibility.asp.

The third and final type of government loan is a *USDA loan*, which is insured by the United States Department of Agriculture. These loans are limited to properties located in rural areas. States and counties have different loan limits. In California, for example, the highest loan amount is offered in Mendocino County: $215,000. These loans also have eligibility income limits. In other words, a person seeking a USDA loan has to have an income that falls below a certain level in order to be eligible for the loan. For people living in certain geographic areas, these loans can be a good solution.

FIRST-TIME HOMEBUYERS

Many clients who come to my company are first-time homebuyers. They are from a diverse set of backgrounds and ages. The one thing that most of them have in common is a concern about interest rates. They are what we in the industry call *shoppers*. They are not familiar with our services; therefore, the first question they ask is, "What is your rate?" As you will see over and over in this book, there is no direct answer to that question.

Many first-time homebuyers have good income but little savings. So, usually, in addition to their down payment, they must cover closing costs and mortgage insurance. For such a borrower, who has little put away but maintains a decent income, an FHA loan is a good fit. It allows the borrower to offer only 3.5 percent as a down payment. Another advantage of the FHA loan program is it allows non-occupant co-borrowers, such as parents or adult children, to add their income during the qualifying process in order to help the borrower acquire a loan.

In contrast to other borrowers, veterans are not required to produce a down payment. Such a loan can be a complete gift, the government's thank-you to military personnel for service. Some cities also have special programs for public servants, such as teachers, police officers, and firefighters. From time to time, major banks offer Community Reimbursement Act (CRA) programs. Participating in a CRA is another way to secure a more affordable loan, as the programs are designed for limited-income borrowers. One major stipulation, though, is that for a CRA loan to be approved, the property must be located within a particular, designated area.

Some time ago I received a call from a young architect, who had been referred to me by a friend of a client. The architect had researched mortgage loans on the Internet, learned the terminology, and emphasized his knowledge of current interest rate ranges (from 3.875 to 4.625 percent). He told me I was the first person he had contacted in reference to obtaining a loan. I replied, "I hope I am also the last one."

When the architect contacted me, he was renting a one-bedroom, rent-controlled apartment for $1,200 per month. He had saved $100,000 and wanted to buy a two-bedroom condominium for about $400,000. He inquired about first-time-buyers programs. Unfortunately, since he had a good income and enough money for the down payment, such programs were not applicable to him. I evaluated his information and determined that presenting a 25 percent down payment would give him a much better rate than a first-time-buyers program would. Since he had enough money saved, this approach made perfect sense.

Next, I calculated his tax benefits in terms of owning versus renting. After adding up all the costs and subtracting all the tax deductions, the total amount of his homeowner payment became $1,600: $400 more than his current rent. However, the architect explained he would need to move into a much bigger place with his fiancée soon, anyway. Renting an apartment comparable to the condo he wanted to purchase would cost him at least $2,000 per month. I suggested that since he now knew what to look for in mortgage options, he could start shopping for the best rate. He told me there would be no need; instead, he said, he trusted me to do a better job. He asked what he needed to do to be pre-approved for a loan. I directed him to my website, where he could fill out his loan application on his own time.

CONFORMING AND JUMBO LOANS

The fixed and adjustable loans sold to Fannie Mae and Freddie Mac are called *conforming loans*. They conform both to specific underwriting guidance and to set loan amounts. (The latter have some variations in Hawaii and Alaska. See the table below.) These loan limits vary, depending on the number of units in a building. When the loan amount for high-cost areas increased, a new category of loans was created. This category included *agency-jumbo*, *jumbo-conforming*, and *high-cost-area-conforming loans*. These programs have higher rates and more restrictive underwriting guidance.

Loan Limits

Conforming-loan limits applied to all conventional mortgages delivered to Fannie Mae in 2012. The Federal Housing Finance

Agency established the high-cost areas, which may vary depending on geographic location and loan origination date.

Maximum Original Principal Balance for Loans Closed in 2012				
Units	Contiguous States, District of Columbia, and Puerto Rico		Alaska, Guam, Hawaii, and the U.S. Virgin Islands	
	General	High-Cost*	General	High-Cost*
1	$417,000	$625,500	$625,500	$938,250
2	$533,850	$800,775	$800,775	$1,201,150
3	$645,300	$967,950	$967,950	$1,451,925
4	$801,950	$1,202,925	$1,202,925	$1,804,375

Source: Fannie Mae Website

JUMBO LOANS

Typically, commercial banks offer loans above agency-jumbo-loan limits, called *jumbos*, which are mostly portfolio loans. Some of these loans can be thirty-year, fixed-rate loans with higher interest rates. The majority of the loans are adjustable and fixed for a short period of time. The below list includes some portfolio lenders' options. Loans can have the following options:

- lending amounts up to $5 million;
- lending amounts up to $1 million with 80 percent LTV;
- cash-out policies up to $500,000;
- debt consolidation, which has buyers pay off debts to qualify;
- reserves, in which only six months are needed;
- interest-only (IO) policies up to $1.5 million;
- non-permitted room additions;
- qualification with a minimum FICO score of 660;
- lines of credit with 70 percent LTV up to $350,000;

- buying land up to ten acres; and
- many more options and solutions.

REVERSE MORTGAGES

Reverse mortgages are designed for people who are sixty-two years of age and older. They are very unlike other types of mortgages. In a typical mortgage scenario, the borrower has a loan that requires regular monthly payments and needs to be repaid over many years, and the lender requires rigorous qualification criteria. In contrast, reverse mortgages are simple and easy. They operate, quite literally, in reverse. As long as the borrower has enough equity in the current loan and continues to reside in the property, he or she can receive a one-time lump sum of money or monthly disbursements. It sounds simple—and it is. There are no credit scores to worry about and no proof of income. The only thing that matters is equity in the property.

Today, only one source is federally regulated, HUD-insured, and available for reverse mortgages: FHA's Home Equity Conversion Mortgage (HECM). Acquisition of an HECM includes upfront fees that become part of the loan's balance, including mortgage insurance. Of course, there is also an interest rate. In this case, the interest accumulates and reduces the property's remaining equity. Since it involves elderly borrowers (and their children), the HECM loan process requires an obligatory counseling session conducted by approved counselors. At the time this book was written, this upfront-only session fee cost $125.

One of my clients, who was born in 1924, has lived in her house since 1952. The home had a small loan attached to it, and she had very little income. After considering her options, she chose an HECM program and received a lump sum, which gave her enough money to enjoy the rest of her life.

One of reverse mortgages' additional advantages is they can be used to purchase property, not just to generate cash from an existing property. In some cases, an eligible borrower can buy a two-, three-, or four-unit building and reside in one of the units without making monthly payments, all while collecting rent from the other units to support his or her own residency.

HARD-MONEY LOANS

When I started in the mortgage business, twenty-nine years ago, mortgage brokers loaned money from their own accounts. These brokers were private individuals; their loans were called *hard-money loans* in order to distinguish them from the *soft-money loans* banks offered. Mortgage brokerage has evolved, but hard-money lenders have remained. Today, typically, hard-money lenders will loan either their own money or investors' money to a borrower who has enough equity built up in a residential or commercial property. The catch is that hard-money lenders charge a higher interest rate than most other lenders. The government recently passed legislation restricting lending hard money to owner-occupied properties. Therefore, to obtain a hard-money loan now, the property must be a rental or used for a business.

Hard-money loans have a lower LTV and higher interest rates and costs. With some exceptions, usually they are offered for a short time, from 6 months to five years. The longer the terms, the higher the rates.

Recently, I arranged two loans. One was for a client who owned a rental property free and clear. While he had resided in the property, he had recently moved out. He decided to pull some equity out of the property. To secure the loan, he had to wait until the property was rented. At that point, I was able to secure a three-year mortgage for him with 50 percent LTV. The loan was at 10 percent interest and cost four points. (See Chapter Five for more detail on points.)

Another case, which took place about two years ago, involved a borrower who owned a number of industrial/commercial buildings in downtown San Francisco. I arranged a $400,000 loan at 11 percent interest for him. However, his lack of cash flow required him to borrow more. He owned another building, which was worth at least $3 million, free and clear. To get his new loan, he needed to pull $175,000 out of his other property. Fortunately, he was able to receive this money within one week. The lender gave him a loan at 11 percent, and he paid four points on the principal.

RESIDENTIAL VERSUS COMMERCIAL

Many of the clients who came to my company for residential mortgages also own apartments or other commercial buildings. Commercial loans use different criteria for underwriting. **The emphasis**

is on the revenue tenants generate. The amount of gross rent, the building's location, and its functionality, determine that building's value.

Commercial-loan down payments need to be higher than residential-loan down payments. In addition, for a property to qualify, the borrower must provide evidence that the commercial income will produce sufficient revenue. Though some lenders advertise an LTV as high as 75 percent, in many cases it is closer to 60 percent or lower. Lenders do make exceptions for Small Business Administration (SBA) loans, for which a down payment can be as low as 10 percent. Those loans are combinations of bank loans, at 50 percent LTV, and SBA loans for the remaining 40 percent. They are designed for buildings with at least 51 percent owner-occupancy.

Commercial banks and credit unions offer commercial loans. Each bank has its own preferences and underwriting guidance. My company always maintains a commercial department, which usually consists of one person who has expertise in commercial underwriting. Because my colleagues and I are also experts in residential lending, we review the borrower's whole portfolio, finding ways to improve his or her overall cash flow. Sometimes, we use money from residential loan financing to pay down commercial obligations.

When our company, Pacific Bay Financial, joined Bay Equity as residential mortgage bankers in 2011, we converted into a commercial mortgage brokerage firm. Brokering a commercial mortgage requires expertise, which we have developed through years of experience. Unlike a residential mortgage brokerage, a commercial mortgage is not heavily regulated. We plan to grow this part of our business by segmenting various types of commercial buildings and attracting bright, young talent.

Due to government regulations, small commercial and community banks are feeling their share of challenges. As a result, they are not consistent in their lending practices. Therefore, we always have to look for new sources to help our clients.

COMMERCIAL LOANS

People are surrounded by commercial properties, such as apartment buildings, office buildings, hotels, hospitals, restaurants, and retail stores. Outside cities are industrial buildings and storage facilities. All of these buildings are financed through commercial loans, which are offered by large commercial or community banks. These banks usually specialize in specific types of properties. Some like to deal in apartment buildings, some focus on special-use real estate (such as medical buildings), and some have good programs for the owner-user. Regardless of the lender, the major underwriting criteria is income the building produces.

These lenders are not concerned so much about the building's owners, although this concept is beginning to change. Instead, they focus on the tenants. Therefore, it is very important that borrowers examine their tenants' sources of income. The tenants are going to be paying rent, and the owners are going to be using that money to make monthly payments. Consider that these loans have typical LTVs of 70 percent or lower. Because their loan amounts are limited by income, apartment building LTVs can be as low as 50 or even 40 percent.

To calculate the loan amount, lenders use actual rent figures minus expenses, which usually are shown in tax returns. Often, these buildings have empty apartments in them. In these instances, lenders deduct about 5 percent for vacancies. They also deduct about

5 percent for management fees, even when an owner manages the building him- or herself. This additional 5 percent is included in case an owner is not able to continue making payments; at that point, the bank will have to hire a building manager when it takes over the building.

Commercial loans are more challenging than residential loans because the tenant or user of the building determines the borrower's ability to support the loan. Recently, we have had a number of cases in which we had to change a building's structure of lease payments to enable the building's owner, our client, to be approved for a loan.

In one of our commercial-loan cases, a client owned a single-user industrial building that was being leased by a furniture distribution company. His bank was concerned that the furniture business was unpredictable and the owner risked losing his tenant. Since commercial loans are usually written for shorter periods of time (such as five, seven, or ten years), the loans are due after the expiration date. This requires a balloon payment. (See Chapter Five for more information on balloon payments.) At that time, the loans have to be either paid off in full or refinanced for another short period. Since the bank could not write this loan, our client had a big problem. His bank recommended he contact us.

What to do? Without income from his tenant, he would not be able to meet his mortgage payments. After analyzing the situation and making calculations, we arrived at the conclusion that if our client lowered his tenant's rent, we would still be able to get him the desired loan amount. We advised him to go back to his tenant and negotiate a rent reduction. Of course, the tenant agreed. This alteration allowed us to repackage the loan and send it to the lender for approval. Everybody won.

In another of our cases, our client, a not-for-profit organization, owned an office building in downtown San Francisco. The building had a reinforced brick foundation and eighty tenants. Many lenders were not interested in lending because of the building's less-than-favorable physical foundation and because it was owned by a not-for-profit organization. Finally, after sending the loan package to eight different banks, we found a lender willing to provide a loan in spite of those things.

Then, however, we were faced with other challenges. For one thing, many of the tenants' leases were not written correctly. We had to work with the owner's accounting firm and review each lease—eighty of them—to create new documents that would be acceptable to the lender. After the appraisal was done, we learned that a major roof repair was needed. We factored this need into the loan amount and negotiated with the lender. Getting the higher loan amount allowed the not-for-profit to fix the building and bring it up to standards.

THE FIVE Cs

E verything I have explained in the book's first few chapters leads to the cornerstone of the mortgage business: the Five Cs.

To understand this concept, think of a mortgage as similar to a car. The average person does not know how his or her car works. He or she just places the key in the ignition and drives. However, every car is a complex mechanism that requires many people to create it. After all that, someone has to sell it. Before a consumer buys a car, he has to make a decision about which car is "the best" for him. Which color? Which accessories? Which price? Which monthly payments? Which dealership?

Mortgages are also complex mechanisms and somebody has to sell them. Since mortgages are so complex, why would anyone be interested in knowing how they work? When people purchase real estate, they expect they will become the proud new owners of a house, condominium, or some other piece of property as soon as their agent hands over the keys.

In reality, it's not so simple. To buy real estate, most buyers need financing. To define the terms of such financing, the mortgage industry commonly uses the Four Cs of Underwriting: capacity, credit, collateral, and capital. These qualities are ranked in order of importance.

I've transformed the Four Cs into the Five Cs. I added one more quality, character, which connects the other four Cs. I also moved collateral to the first position. Because of recent changes in the economy, collateral has become the most important factor in obtaining a mortgage. Knowing the Five Cs and how they depend on one another might help a potential borrower find the right mortgage and obtain it with fewer challenges.

To understand the Five Cs and how they are connected to each other, let's use a house as an example. A house needs a foundation: the collateral, which is our first C. It also needs walls, or capacity, which is our second C. It needs windows and doors, or credit, which is our third C. It needs plumbing, electricity, and heating, the combination of which creates capital, our fourth C. In addition, of course, it needs a roof: its character, which is our fifth C. When one of the Cs is lacking, weak, or damaged, the house cannot properly function. The same is true of a mortgage.

In this chapter, I demonstrate why it is important to understand the Five Cs, what the Five Cs are, and how your knowledge of them can increase your ability to find a great mortgage.

Let's begin with the interest rate, the prime concern of just about every borrower. The interest rate is a measure of the risk that the lender assumes. Each C has an effect on what kind of program a borrower can qualify for and, by extension, the approved interest rate.

All Five Cs are interconnected and can be measured:
- Collateral has an LTV role.
- Capacity is the income you are required to have to qualify for a loan.
- Credit is impacted by your credit scores.
- Capital is your money in the bank or your investments.
- Character, or characteristics of a transaction, affects underwriting guidance.

At the same time, a "plus" in one of the Five Cs can help offset a "minus" in one of the others. A lower LTV can offset a lower credit score, for example. Lower ratios can affect your ability to obtain a mortgage, while a certain loan amount will determine a specific interest rate. Note that I mentioned the interest rate last, because that rate can be determined only after examining all Five Cs.

The character of this transaction determines which underwriting guidance will be used in the loan approval process. Again, it determines the rate. Remember, usually lenders only talk about the Four Cs. Their model is based on the borrowers' ability to repay mortgages. However, the fifth C of the 5 Cs—character—**defines the characteristics of the transaction. It dictates not only the program and the interest rate, but also the lender who can approve the mortgage request.**

At the same time, there are instances in which some of the Cs are absent. In those cases, banks cannot approve a loan. Instead, borrowers need to find creative solutions. To show you how it can be done, I want to share how my wife and I bought our first house.

---

*In April 1984, my wife and I bought our first house in the United States. The price was $225,000. The only C we had at the time was character. In the mortgage business, **character** describes a transaction's circumstances. At the time, our family consisted of my wife, our two daughters, and my wife's mother. We had $10,000 in savings left over from the sale of our house in Israel. Like many other immigrants, we wanted to become part of the American Dream. I knew we would not be able to get a mortgage from a bank. However, that did not stop us from looking for a house. Just six months before we began looking, I* had started my new job in the mortgage company and received a few commission checks.

A friend who sold real estate told us about a house that had been taken off the market because the owner could not sell it for her desired price. We drove by and liked both the house and the area. I suggested arranging a meeting with the owner. This is not commonly done, but in my life, according to my philosophy, "no" is the first step to "yes."

We scheduled the meeting. When the time for the meeting arrived, our whole family showed up. The owner, a widow whose children had grown up in the house, liked our family so much that she agreed to sell her house to us and to sell it for less than she had originally wanted. On top of that, she agreed to carry the mortgage for a year. We just needed to come up with a down payment of $40,000. Well, we were $30,000 short.

Russians have a saying that translates, roughly, to this piece of wisdom: "You do not need a hundred rubles if you have a hundred friends." At that time, I did not have a hundred friends, but I did have six. I asked each of them to lend me $5,000 for one year. Our real-estate agent even loaned me his commission. My wife was nervous for the whole year. How would we be able to pay back $30,000 to six different people and refinance our mortgage? I did not know how we would do it either. Fortunately, a year later our house had appreciated in value. After World Savings Bank agreed to give us our first mortgage, we were able to repay everyone. We are still friends with the individuals who helped us purchase our first house, which became our home, and who would help us many more times in the years to come.

As the years progressed and our house continued to appreciate, we proceeded to "milk it" more and more. We took out loans against the house's value and used the money to repair it and to buy more properties. Years later, we even used money from our house to help our daughter. At one point, our house was appraised at close to $2 million.

It could probably be sold today for at least $1.5 million. The balance of our mortgage is $530,000, and we have monthly payments of $1,300. Twenty-eight years ago, when we started our real-estate journey, we had only one C and could not obtain a regular mortgage. Today, through patience and perseverance, we have all the Five Cs: collateral, which amounts to $1 million in equity; capacity, in that we earn enough to pay our mortgage; credit, which is excellent (I have never made a late payment, even in the toughest times), capital, which is our money in the bank; and character, of which we have plenty.

It was not always this way. In 1993, our mortgage was close to $600,000, but the value of our house was about the same. At that time, the mortgage business was very slow. We had difficulty making our mortgage payments. I actually asked my wife if she thought we should move out and live in one of our rental apartments. We would have had to sell our house for less than what we owed. My wife refused. I had no choice but to work harder and to pray. The mortgage business rebounded, we still live here, and our children each have their own room when they visit. So the lesson is this: in tougher times, be patient and keep going.

COLLATERAL

While each C affects a lender's decision about whether or not to grant a loan, without collateral there can be no mortgage. There is often confusion about the difference between *collateral* and *equity*, and it may seem logical to state that they are essentially the same thing. This is not true. Equity, quite simply, is the difference between a property's value and the loan amount. As real estate appreciates, especially over a long period of time, equity grows. In some lucky years, appreciation has gone as high as 30 percent.

In the past, borrowers who accumulated equity in their homes and wanted to refinance could not understand why their loan applications were denied. "After all," they reasoned, "the bank has the collateral. If I am not able to make payments, they can have my house." Now, after millions of foreclosures on properties with no equity left, we are seeing a different picture. When real-estate property is sold on the free market, equity is the thing that matters most.

Net equity is what is left after the mortgage, deferred interest, delinquent property taxes, other liens and costs, and agent commissions are subtracted from the sales price.

If a borrower stops making mortgage payments, a property will go into foreclosure for less than the loan amount. Often, foreclosed properties need repairs, which result in extra costs. Additional legal costs are also associated with foreclosures. Because of all these factors, often banks are willing to sell a foreclosed property in what is called a *short sale*. They are willing to be flexible about the sale price in order to sell the property as quickly as possible. This flexibility allows banks to reduce their "dead assets," or foreclosed properties, which only other top-performing assets can offset. In other words, a chain is only as strong as its weakest link. A foreclosed property is a weak link in a bank's chain. Therefore, in order to create collateral for the bank, and show that his or her property is less likely to become a weak link, a borrower needs to have a substantial down payment.

Lenders measure collateral based on the LTV. The higher the LTV, the less collateral there is, and therefore, the more risk there is. To determine the amount of the collateral, lenders use appraisal reports, which are subjective. Humans, who work for specific companies that have their own unique cultures, make these reports.

In preparing an appraisal report, appraisers need to inspect the property, measure it, draw the floor plan, establish square footage, and take photographs. They need to comment on the property's condition and log any improvements, even if those improvements were made prior to current homeownership. If the property is a condominium, any pending lawsuits need to be mentioned. Often property owners, especially those who have made significant improvements, believe that their property is worth more than the number at which the appraiser can arrive.

Becoming a good appraiser requires many years of practice, knowledge of the geographical area, and local conditions. Appraisers use subjective information, such as "similar properties" sold within six months in the general neighborhood, to arrive at their conclusions. In diverse cities, such as San Francisco, those comparisons are not always easy to find. In other words, sometimes it is hard to compare apples to apples accurately. When your property is on the line, you don't want the appraiser to compare your apple to a nearby orange.

Take our house, for example. It was built in 1929 and is located on a corner. It has two garages, which have entrances from different streets. When we moved in, one of the rooms downstairs had only one window. It served as a storage space and contained a huge antique heater. Another room, which was in between the garages, had a bar and a spot for a laundry connection.

Over the years, we changed all of that. In the storage room, we opened up one more window, moved out the old furnace, and built a bathroom with a shower. This room became our eldest daughter's room for some time; today, it serves as my study and is where I wrote this book.

The middle room became my wife's art studio, and we built a separate laundry room. All of these rooms have served us well through the years. Although our contractor obtained the proper permits for construction, they were never submitted for general remodeling approval and consequently are not reflected in City Hall records. As a result, in the official record, our house is listed as 2,800 square feet, instead of its actual 3,600 square feet.

In situations like the one described here, an appraiser needs to be knowledgeable and creative. Many old buildings, such as those in San Francisco, have similar situations that cannot be easily categorized. Luckily, buyers look at houses as a whole, considering all of their unique characteristics. However, these quirks and qualities can definitely affect a home's appraised value.

Another issue connected with collateral is insurance coverage. Insurance companies insure buildings based on square footage, since this number offers a clear-cut way to determine replacement value in case of a disaster. Consequently, buildings that do not have clearly defined work plans or proof of improvement projects might be underinsured. Establishing accurate property value is challenging to say the least. This has been especially true lately, since so many property values have gone down.

Nick and Mary bought a single-family house in a nice neighborhood. The house had a large garage and a separate storage space. Nick, who worked as a contractor, converted part of the garage and storage space into a one-bedroom apartment with a separate entrance. He received permits for the work without showing the kitchen plan. After remodeling, Nick and Mary rented out the unit to help subsidize their mortgage payments.

There are many properties like this one in San Francisco. Some of these "in-law units," in which extended family members live on the same property, were built without any permits at all. This type of remodeling creates a double problem for the appraiser. Even though it may have wonderful features, the property has to be appraised for less than those features are worth if they were added without permits. When the property is sold, buyers look at the property's total condition. However, lenders will not be able to use the unwarranted space's value in their calculations.

CAPACITY

The ability to make monthly payments is called *capacity*. To measure this ability, lenders can use one of two ratios. The first ratio takes into account total monthly payments plus taxes and insurance. We call this ratio *PITI*, which stands for principal and interest, taxes and insurance. If mortgage insurance (MI) is part of the picture, it also gets factored in. In the case of financing a condominium or townhouse, usually a monthly fee required by the homeowners' association (HOA) must also be included. This fee, also called a *monthly assessment*, pays a single owner's share of building insurance, general upkeep, and any amenities, such as an exercise room or a rooftop deck. The first ratio is calculated by dividing monthly PITI payments by monthly income. To calculate the second ratio, the "Debt to Income Ratio," monthly liabilities, such as debt payments and student loans, are added to the PITI and then the sum is divided by monthly income. This ratio is used to obtain the amount of assets a person needs in order to qualify for a loan.

Capacity is often the sore point in underwriting. Since the lender needs to insure itself, they try to be careful and selective in who they will grant money to. As we'll see, capacity and collateral are very tightly connected. The LTV has a direct effect on the ratio lenders are going to use. For example, as a general rule, if the LTV is 60 percent, the ratio can be as high as 45 percent. If the LTV is 95 percent, the ratio cannot exceed 38 percent.

Meanwhile, however, there can be an exception to the rule that depends on the fifth C: the transaction's character. Since income is an important part of the equation, it is critical to know how to calculate that income correctly. Borrowers often shop for mortgages on the Internet, using provided mortgage calculators. This is a waste of time: borrowers do not know exactly how much income the lenders will consider. Many sources of income—including commissions, bonuses, and hourly and self-employed income—are only taken into consideration if they are reported in tax returns for at least two years. Some borrowers who receive a monthly salary and a W2 form might work for an agency; if so, they must provide a two-year history.

Changing income streams can affect borrowers in a variety of ways. One of our clients worked for PG&E, the electric company, for seven years. To save on benefits, PG&E offered to make her an independent contractor. This meant she continued doing the same type of work, but received higher wages. Without realizing it, she became a self-employed person. That meant that after only two years, she was able to qualify for a mortgage by showing an apparently higher income.

In another example, I worked with my long-term clients Nick and Mary to refinance their mortgage. When they approached me about refinancing, I was very happy to find out that Nick had just been offered a job after two years of unemployment. Despite the fact that he had been employed in the same profession for more than thirty years, the two years of unemployment created a problem for loan qualification. We waited until he received his first paycheck (about a month) before submitting the loan. However, when we submitted the loan we found out the underwriting guidance had changed. For one thing, in order for Nick's income to count, we would need to wait until he worked for at least six months with his new employer. For another, even though Nick and Mary received rent money from the apartment Nick had built, this income stream could not be counted in loan proceedings because the apartment was not legally a separate unit. Therefore, we waited for six months. Luckily, by that time interest rates went down, and I obtained a new mortgage for them.

Ironically, considering these complexities, a student who finds a job can qualify for a mortgage right away as long as he or she can provide the proper educational documents and has a new job that pays a monthly salary.

Capacity is also tightly connected with credit. Suppose a married couple wanted to buy property together. If one spouse has a problem with credit, that problem can cut down the couple's joint score. This cut can drastically affect their interest rate or even prevent them from obtaining a mortgage altogether. In these cases, we often recommend the spouse with the credit problems be entirely removed from the loan. The challenge then becomes figuring out how the remaining spouse can qualify for a loan with limited income.

There are many factors to consider. When we work with our clients, we evaluate every possible option in order to arrive at the right combination of the Five Cs.

In some instances, relatives can cosign for each other. In these cases, income and liabilities are combined. For instance, Eugene, his wife, and their two children recently moved back to San Francisco from Arizona. They had lived in Arizona for four years while Eugene tried to develop his own business. When his wife, Olga, was offered a better job in the Bay Area, the family returned to California and resided in Olga's parents' apartment. This was the type of apartment that is not even supposed to have a kitchen. Therefore, Eugene and Olga were ready to start looking for their first house. I helped them secure an FHA loan.

They found a house they liked and wanted to buy it. Eugene and Olga were ready to spend up to $480,000. At the time of purchase, Eugene expected to start working at a new, salaried job one month later. The family wanted to make an offer on a house right away, but Olga's income alone would not be enough for them to qualify. Understanding this, Eugene offered to use his mother as a cosigner for their mortgage, which solved the problem. Parents cosigning mortgages for their children is a relatively common practice. Children even sometimes cosign for their parents.

Only a few programs allow family members to cosign mortgages. One of them is the FHA. However, even FHA loans don't always permit cosigners, depending on the circumstances of all parties involved. Remember, lenders not only combine the cosigners' incomes; they also combine the cosigners' expenses and liabilities.

Cosigners' liabilities, such as house payments, often outweigh the added income's benefit.

Another issue with cosigning is paying the mortgage on time. If the person who owns the property fails to do so and suffers a late payment fee, everyone's credit is affected.

Recently, my clients Maegan and Leo approached me. They wanted to buy a house together. Unfortunately, Leo owned a previous property that had been foreclosed. He had to wait seven years before he could qualify for a new mortgage. Maegan's income was not sufficient to qualify for a mortgage on her own. To solve the problem, Maegan suggested adding her adult son, Michael, to the loan application. Michael earned a salary that would allow the family to qualify for the loan. However, after running his credit report, we discovered that his middle credit score was 662, and we needed it to be 700. To increase his score and qualify for the loan, Michael had to pay down his debts, for which he needed an extra $20,000.

One of our clients who had cosigned on a car purchase for his wife's son discovered a similar unfortunate truth. When the man came to us to refinance his mortgage, we ran his credit report. To his amazement and disappointment, he found that his credit score had dropped because the young man had not made some of his car payments on time. According to the loan's terms, our client was "responsible." It took our client six months to remove this blemish from his credit report and increase his score. Fortunately, during the interim the interest rate dropped even more. When he finally refinanced, our client improved his payment.

Low interest rates also help to qualify buyers. A major part of the ratio calculation is the mortgage payment or the principle and interest (PI). If it is a fixed rate, then the calculation can be straightforward. Most mortgages are amortized (that is, paid off) in thirty years. Some clients prefer a shorter loan, such as one for twenty or fifteen years, which has a lower interest rate. However, a shorter loan's monthly payments will be higher and qualifying for it will be more difficult. When it comes to qualifying for adjustable loans, which are fixed for five or seven years, lenders add 2 percent to a five-year loan's initial rate. Simultaneously, a loan fixed for seven years is qualified at the initial rate. Interest-only (IO) loans have lower monthly payments but are qualified at high rates. Understanding all of these issues makes a huge difference in finding the right mortgage.

Another important consideration related to capacity is debt. Debt is part of credit, since it appears on credit reports, and it is very important to know how to deal with debt. As I discussed earlier, debts can both affect a mortgage ratio and lower credit scores. Debt can make or break a loan.

There are two types of debt: *revolving*, as with department-store credit cards, and *installment*, as with car payments and mortgages. Both kinds get factored into mortgage applications. During refinancing, some lenders allow revolving debt to be paid down in order to affect the application process positively.

Jane and her son owned a house together. Jane was unable to work; she lived on disability payments and obviously had limited income. This house was her primary residence and she wanted to refinance it. To apply for refinancing, we needed to include both owners' incomes.

Jane's credit score was quite high. However, her son had accumu-
lated a great deal of debt. To take advantage of a low interest rate of
3.875 percent, we locked the rate in for sixty days. During this period, Jane
paid off her son's credit card. Still, we needed to wait a month until a new
credit report reflected desirable results. We were creative, but the solution
still took time.

I received a phone call recently from a client who owned a property
with an interest rate of 6 percent. He inquired if he could get a better
rate. He told me about the medical problems his wife was having, which
meant he was unable to work full time. Instead, he was self-employed
and, due to his many available tax write-offs, did not show significant
income on his tax returns. All this could have made refinancing very
difficult. Then he said the magic words: "But I have a very good credit
score." When it comes to credit, there are two categories of people in the
world: those who care about their credit history and those who do not. I
hope you belong to the first group.

In the 1990s, the mortgage business was very slow. My wife is in charge of the money in our company and in our personal life. Juggling monthly payments and handling all the finances needed to keep a company afloat is a very difficult task. One day, when I was checking our credit report for yet another refinancing, I noticed our car payment and another bill were both thirty days late. I do not remember ever being so upset as I was about that discovery. From that day forward, no matter how difficult it was, we always paid our bills in full and on time.

CREDIT SCORES

A credit report is the bloodline of mortgage success or failure. The majority of credit issuers commonly use the credit scoring system called a *FICO score.* The Fair Isaac Company developed the FICO, which is based on mathematical calculations and uses information from various consumer sources to establish credit levels that fall between 300 and 850 points. To receive a credit score, you can use one of three credit-rating agencies: Experion, Equifax, or TransUnion. All use a FICO scoring system, though it may appear under a different name.

The credit rating agencies are not perfect. Sometimes, there are mistakes on the credit report, which affect scores. Everyone should check his or her credit scores once a year. This process can be done free of charge. Since it takes time to correct mistakes, I recommend my clients check their credit reports at least three months before applying for a mortgage. Checking a client's credit report is one of the first things we do in my business. The credit company we use gives us all three credit scores and a complete credit history. Only after we receive these reports can we determine the right course of action for the client.

The following table shows how a credit score can affect a potential mortgage's interest rate and LTV.

Credit Scores Vs. Rate

Mid Credit Score	LTV	PAR Rates - Borrower Paid Compensation (BPC)												
		ARM								FIXED			Second Position	
		First Position								First Position				
		ARM Margin	1/1	3/1	3/1 IO	5/1	5/1 IO	7/1	10/1	15 year	20 year	30 year	15 year	20 year
740+	75%[2]	2.20	2.20	2.35	2.50	2.75	3.00	3.15	3.50	3.35	3.65	4.05	7.35	7.50
	80%[1]	2.30	2.30	2.45	-	2.75	-	3.15	3.50	3.35	3.65	4.05	-	-
720-739	75%[2]	2.20	2.20	2.50	2.75	2.75	3.00	3.15	3.50	3.35	3.65	4.05	7.35	7.50
	80%	2.50	2.50	2.60	-	2.75	-	3.15	3.50	3.35	3.65	4.05	-	-
680-719	70%[1]	2.50	2.50	2.65	2.85	2.90	3.15	3.30	3.65	3.55	3.85	4.15	7.70	7.85
	75%	2.55	2.55	2.75	-	3.00	-	3.40	3.75	3.55	3.95	4.25	-	-
	80%	2.60	2.66	2.85	-	3.10	-	3.50	3.85	3.65	4.05	4.35	-	-
660-679	70%	3.30	3.30	3.50	-	3.55	-	3.70	4.00	3.70	4.00	4.30	-	-
	75%	3.35	3.35	3.55	-	3.60	-	3.85	4.15	3.75	4.15	4.45	-	-

[1] 3/1 IO and 5/1 IO ARMs allowed up to 65% LTV with minimum 700 credit score required.
[2] Second position maximum 70% LTV / 70% CLTV.

Source: U.S. Bank (Non Agency Rates for California) via
https://www.usbank.com/cgi_w/cfm/mortgagebrokers/logon/display_PDF.cfm?pdfName=U.S._Bank_Wholesale_Rates_AZ_CA_FL_MI_NV.pdf)

While we are working on clients' loans, we warn them not to do anything drastic with their credit unless they tell us about it. That's because lenders often check credit on their own, even after they receive a loan package, before funding. It can be extremely frustrating when, toward the end of the application process, something like a late payment pops up. Something like this can drop a client's credit score by as much as 100 points and ruin his or her opportunity to get a mortgage. When this happens, we have to start all over again. The client needs to remove the blemish and that takes time. Only then can we resubmit the loan with a completely new set of documents.

Recently, this very scenario happened to one of my clients. A simple late payment stalled the whole process and sent us back to step one. A late payment or some other negative credit circumstance can also cause an increase in credit card interest rates. Don't be late with your credit card payments, especially when you are in the process of applying for a mortgage.

One of the secrets of increasing a credit score is paying down credit-card balances. Here is a basic rule to follow: the amount of debt must not exceed 30 percent of the highest balance. For example, if a high balance is $9,000, the debt amount must not exceed $3,000. I used this calculation when I recommended that Mary's son, Michael, pay off $20,000 of his debt. **The payment has to be calculated and applied to each account. After the payoff is reported to the credit companies, we can run a new credit report again a month later.** The more open accounts with zero or low balances, the better. Old open accounts are better than new ones. I advise clients not to close accounts, while remembering not to abuse those accounts.

Some borrowers have no credit history, having used cash for all of their prior purchases. While using cash might be prudent, it is no help to a person's consumer credit score. Instead, people who lack credit history can offer their utility bills—telephone, gas, electric, and even insurance bills—as proof they will be reliable borrowers. Only reverse mortgages do not require credit scores.

CAPITAL

We all know cash is king. While I have refinanced a limited number of properties that were purchased with cash, the majority of real-estate buyers cannot buy property outright. Even those who buy with cash often prefer to diversify investments and apply for a mortgage. Only VA and USDA loans can be granted without any down payment. All other loans require borrowers to demonstrate availability of capital for a down payment. In the case of FHA loans, the down payment can be as little as 3.5 percent. **The bigger the down payment, the better the interest rate and mortgage terms**. Down payments create LTV, which is the measurement of the lender's risk.

For a purchase, borrowers need to have money for the down payment, closing costs, property taxes, insurance (that is, the cost of ownership), and reserves. While the down payment can come from different sources, the most common is money from a savings account at a bank. This source must be verified by showing at least two months of banking statements. Some people use other sources to supplement the down payment, such as investments, liquidated jewelry, and coin or stamp collections. To verify these kinds of resources, a lender needs a letter of evaluation plus an official appraisal. The financial source can be a gift from relatives, too. In such case, the lender requires a gift letter and statements as proof the funds are available. Having 20 percent available for a down payment eliminates the need for mortgage insurance. To meet this limit, money can be borrowed from relatives and paid to them at the same interest rate the bank charges for the mortgage, creating a win-win situation.

I met Margaret in my office on a Sunday afternoon. She was referred to me by her friend, our former client. During our earlier phone conversation, she had told me she had a good income, very little savings, and some debt. We discussed different options. One was to borrow money from her sister.

Then, another potential solution emerged. Margaret mentioned she had an individual retirement account (IRA) with a significant amount of money in it. In two months, she would turn fifty-nine and a half, the age when one can withdraw money from an IRA. With that potential influx of cash, I realized she already had enough money for the down payment, or 25 percent of the condominium's purchase price of $500,000, without the need to borrow from her sister or anyone else. I connected Margaret with a trustworthy real-estate agent to help her find a condominium.

Given the down payment she could afford, Margaret could also easily handle the monthly payment, which, including taxes and assessments, would be $1,400. That number was less than her current monthly rent. Margaret planned to work fifteen more years, until she turned seventy-five, and wanted to save some money during that time. Based on this information, I recommended she take a fifteen-year, fixed-rate loan instead of a thirty-year loan. Although payments would be higher, the interest rate would be lower. Plus, her payments would still be $500 less than her monthly rent payments had been. (I also recommended she use her tax refund to pay off her credit card debt.)

A retirement plan, such as a 401(k), can also be used for a down payment. An account holder can borrow up to 50 percent of the total amount. Sometimes, these sources can be used to establish a reserve account, too.

At the beginning of a loan transaction, the lender or mortgage broker needs to prepare a good faith estimate (GFE), which shows the amount of money needed for the closing costs, the cost of one year's worth of insurance and property tax, and the first month's loan payment. The closing costs can be rolled into the down payment and paid as part of that total amount. If borrowers choose to pay points to lower their interest rate, this amount is added to the initial costs, too.

Sometimes the seller or builder of a new home agrees to pay for closing costs. A borrower's choice of a higher interest rate can lower the total amount needed at closing. During refinancing, closing costs can be added to the loan amount if the property has enough equity. These closing costs can also be folded into the interest rate. While I was writing this book, for example, many of our clients refinanced their mortgages at close to 4 percent with no out-of-pocket closing costs.

Strangely, cash cannot be used for a down payment. Many years ago I helped a client, who is originally from China, fill out a loan application. We had met at her home to discuss her funding options. I asked her where her money for the down payment would be coming from. She disappeared into her bedroom and came back with a wad of rolled-up newspaper. When she opened it, she revealed about $25,000 in cash. I told her that that might not be enough. She said, "I have more."

That method doesn't work any longer. The only way to get a loan is to demonstrate that you have funds in established accounts. Today, banks are more conservative; they have to follow the Patriot Act Guidelines to prevent money laundering and avoid any other undocumented sources of capital.

CHARACTER

Every mortgage loan has its own characteristics, circumstances, limitations, challenges, and creative solutions. In each case, character is essentially defined by the lender's underwriting guidance. As a mortgage professional, my job is to evaluate and understand borrowers' circumstances; it's also my job to find the right lender and the best way to put a loan package together for each client.

---

*Recently, I received a call from a real-estate agent with whom I regularly work. His client wanted to make a $975,000 offer on a condominium in a two-unit building. As a doctor working in a Kaiser hospital, the client was eligible to receive down-payment assistance (DPA) in the amount of 10 percent of the sales price. On top of that, he had saved his own 10 percent for the down payment. This combination meant he was capable of entering into what is called an **80–10–10** mortgage transaction. The amount of the loan was $780,000, which made it a jumbo loan. Our challenge was to find a lender who would accept the DPA. Luckily, we did.*

In another instance, I received a call from a different real-estate agent who had heard about my reputation as a problem solver. The agent's client wanted to buy a house with a mortgage of $400,000. The client could put 35 percent down, but since he was self-employed, he did not show enough income to qualify.

Fortunately, there are a few lenders that offer loans fixed for three, five, or seven years and do not require proof of income. One bank that I work with from time to time, and which the real-estate agent knew about, had recently increased its requirements to 40 percent down. The question was whether we could find another bank that would require only 35 percent. After making a few calls, I found one. To obtain a loan would cost the borrower two points in addition to regular closing costs. Problem solved.

However, if there is no other choice, a client needs to make a decision either to go with the offer or not. In other words, the client has to decide whether or not to buy.

In another recent transaction, I helped a client who was going through a divorce. As part of the settlement, she had to give her ex-husband $100,000. She owned a home and a rental property, had a good job and savings, and her credit score was more than 720. Unfortunately, her qualifying ratio was higher than 60 percent, primarily because of the deductions she was allowed from her rental property. Her home did not have enough lendable equity. Therefore, we had to refinance the rental property. To do that we needed to find a lending source that would not include her personal income in its formula.

After the property was appraised at $600,000, the bank gave her a loan for $300,000, which was a 50 percent LTV. This amount was enough to refinance her loan, plus give the necessary cash, and the solution kept

*her monthly payment almost the same as it had been before. This was
the last cash-out refinancing transaction this bank ever did. Since then,
no banks that offer non-stated income loans have offered cash-outs.*

CONNECTION BETWEEN THE 5 Cs

Government control over the mortgage business has created an environment in which large players (such as Citibank, Bank of America,
MetLife, Wells Fargo, and ING) have pulled out from the mortgage-
brokerage side of the business. This was unfortunate, since these
companies had offered a diversity of products to satisfy variations of
the Five Cs. As a result, many borrowers were trapped; we could not
help them buy new properties or lower their monthly payments.

Previously, our company had been approved by and was able to
use about a hundred lenders. During the economic downturn's three
years, the majority of these lenders disappeared. As the new mortgage
reality emerged, some banks survived. Today, about thirty lenders
approve us. When we select a lender, we have to decide how the Five
Cs will correlate and how that correlation will affect the final result.
We have to find the best scenario and then the best interest rate.

Each lender's rate changes daily. Sometimes, points enter the
equation and change the rates even more. To help us do our job well,
we use a software program called *Loan Sifter*. All lenders deposit their
information into this program daily. This software allows us to track
the changes on a day-to-day basis and recognize the changing cor-
relations of the Five Cs.

Here is a real-life example of how the Five Cs relate to each other. One of my frequent clients referred his sister, Sophia, to me. Sophia and her fiancé, Richard, were moving to the Bay Area from Atlanta. Sophia had a good job; plus, since her work could be done primarily online, she could live anywhere in the world. Richard also had a good job; he was a consultant for a major bank that had business in San Francisco. Since Sophia's parents and brother lived in the Bay Area, it made perfect sense for her and Richard to relocate there. The couple had $100,000 of capital to use as a down payment.

On the surface, it looked like getting a mortgage for these two would be easy. Then, challenges started to appear. Both Sophia and Richard had owned homes with mortgages in Georgia. While Richard earned a good income, as mentioned above, he was an independent contractor who had less than two years in his current position. Unfortunately, in spite of having many years of other work experience, high earnings, and other economic benefits, his income could not be used for the current loan's qualifying purposes. To complicate matters, he had sold his property as a short sale, which had a negative impact on his credit history. This took Richard out of the picture; instead, Sophia had to qualify for the loan based on her own income. They wanted to buy a house for about $700,000. In some areas of the country, this amount of money would be enough to buy a castle. In San Francisco, it buys a two-bedroom, two-bath home.

Besides their income constraints, Sophia and Richard also had a limitation in terms of how much they had available for a down payment. I recommended they aim for a loan amount of up to $625,000, which would offer them a low, thirty-year fixed rate. Since we did not know when the loan would actually close, I could only estimate the rate. The cash they had was enough for a down payment of 10 percent plus closing costs, and Sophia had a 401(k) plan that could be used for the reserves. Just when we thought we had it figured out, we encountered another obstacle. I found out Sophia's house in Georgia was being rented, but it had rented to the current tenants for less than two years.

Since conventional underwriting guidelines do not count rent for less than two years as income, we had to run new calculations. This increased Sophia and Richard's debt ratio to more than 46 percent, which was not acceptable. Because their down payment was less than 20 percent, the loan also required mortgage insurance. Adding mortgage insurance would increase their monthly payment. Thus, they would require even more for the down payment.

We needed a new solution. One option was this: we could increase the down payment to 20 percent in order to eliminate mortgage insurance. We could use Sophia's 401(k) funds, from which she could borrow 50 percent, and we could ask relatives for help. Lenders require at least 5 percent of a down payment to be the borrower's own money. The balance can be a gift from close relatives, but it cannot be a loan, as that would increase liability. A gift letter from the relative satisfies the lender's requirements.

However, we had another possible solution. If the rental property in Georgia's mortgage balance equaled 70 percent of the property's value, the lenders would accept the rental income. In other words, lenders would consider it in the application process, even though the income stream was less than two years old. This was a big question mark, since Georgia's real estate values had dropped. In spite of all these issues, I did not give up. After an extensive search, I found a solution. Based on all of the new information we had collected, along with credit reports showing a credit score of more than 729, we were able to submit an application for pre-approval to the lender.

It is easy to see that all of the Five Cs are connected to one another. In certain circumstances, they can work together or compensate for one another on a borrower's behalf. They are among the most important factors in any potential real-estate transaction.

THE BEST RATE

One of the most frequent suggestions in books and articles offering mortgage advice is **to shop for the best interest rate**. There are endless sources of materials available for mortgage professionals and potential borrowers to compare one quote with another. To top it off, government regulation requires loan originators to offer borrowers three choices.

All of this sounds like a good idea, but shopping for interest rates is flawed. First of all, there is no way to quote a rate accurately before evaluating all Five Cs. The problem does not end there. The only way a rate can be guaranteed is if it is locked in for a specific number of days: fifteen, twenty-one, twenty-five, thirty, forty-five, sixty, or, in the case of new home construction, even longer. The more days the rate is locked in, the higher it becomes. A fifteen-day lock is possible only when the lender receives all the required documents, the loan is approved, and all that remains is **funding and recording**. A sixty-day lock is used either when interest rates are low, and lenders are so slammed they cannot underwrite a loan fast enough, or when there are problems with some aspects of an application—a low credit score, for example—that take time to fix.

Margie and Dan decided to apply for a new loan. They wanted a thirty-year, fixed-rate loan at 3.875 percent with no out-of-pocket closing costs. This meant that the loan amount would not change and no extra money would be needed for the closing. They had a first mortgage and a line of credit (L/C). To apply for this kind of loan, we needed to have the first loan approved and then apply for subordination of the L/C. This required significant time. We could not accomplish it in thirty days. To ensure the transaction's completion, we needed to lock in the rate for sixty days, but this would not give us the desired results. The best solution was to float the rate (that is, to work on the loan application without locking it in). This was risky, since rates can go any direction and can change a few times a day. At one point, as we worked on the loan, we could have locked in the rate for forty-five days at 3.875 percent, but we did not, and the next day the rate went up. My clients were upset.

Meanwhile, Margie and Dan's bank called and offered to give them the rate they wanted. I suggested that they go forward with the bank's offer while we continued our process. This was a gamble. I prayed that by the time we were approved, the interest rates would come down and we would be able to lock in the rate for fifteen days. In the end, it turned out that the bank was misleading Margie and Dan. Meanwhile, interest rates came down again, and we were able to close the loan. The client was happy, and I earned my commission.

The interest rate depends to a large degree on each transaction's character. Some lenders might offer slightly higher rates but are able to approve a riskier loan (remember Nick and Mary's story and the extra unit they built). Sometimes clients start with one idea and change their mind after doing some research. Obviously, this changes the interest rate.

When a long-term client, Bill, bought his house, I was able to get him a $900,000 loan. This loan was fixed for seven years and had a rate of 4.75 percent. When interest rates dropped, Bill asked me to refinance his adjustable mortgage. He wanted to move to a long-term, thirty-year fixed loan. The day we had our phone conversation, I discovered I could get him the same rate he already had: 4.75 percent for thirty years instead of seven. Then I told him he could also get another seven-year loan at 3.25 percent, which would save him $500 per month in payments. Guess which option he chose.

When a mortgage is a jumbo loan (that is, more than $625,000), the best rates are offered on loans that are fixed for five or seven years and become adjustable afterward (ARMs). Jumbo loans fixed for ten years are priced higher and are not as popular. Personally, my wife and I chose an adjustable mortgage with a rate of 2.8 percent for our home. We chose to refinance and move to this loan a few years ago, when the mortgage business tanked. This served us very well, since we needed to keep our mortgage payments as low as possible. Our only fixed-rate mortgage has a rate of 6.75 percent and is on one of our rental properties. Unfortunately, the value of that property has dropped, and we have not been able to refinance it. The only way to resolve a problem of this sort is to try the HARP 2 Program, which I'll describe later on in the book.

INTEREST TAX DEDUCTION

Mortgage payments include principal and interest, which can save homeowners money via tax deduction. Often, the ability to take such deductions is considered one of home ownership's greatest benefits. At the beginning of each year, lenders send borrowers a statement that details the amount of interest paid on the loan over the course of the previous year. The statement is used by the tax preparer, and the amount of deduction depends on the borrower's tax bracket. There are also limits on the amount of permissible deductions.

If you are considering buying a home, you can use a tax deduction calculation to establish the feasibility of owning versus renting. For example, suppose the loan is for $417,000 at 3.875 percent, amortized over thirty years. The monthly principal and interest payment is $1,961, while the interest portion of that amount is $1,347. The tax reduction, at 35 percent, amounts to $471. So, effectively, the monthly cost to the borrower is $1,508.

To compare that cost to rent, you need to divide the total amount of taxes and insurance by twelve months and prorate it. That's because the interest diminishes each month, as the principal of the mortgage is paid down.

The *interest rate* is the cost of the mortgage loan over a period of time. To lower the rate, part of the cost can be paid up front through the use of a point, or points. Points are also referred to as loan origination fees, loan discounts, or discount points. A single point equals 1 percent of the total loan amount. For example, if the loan amount is $300,000, a point is worth $3,000. In a "buy down" of the interest rate, the point becomes the interest and is subsequently deductible. Depending on which tax bracket they are in when they file their taxes, borrowers can deduct the points. Some borrowers also choose to pay points during refinancing.

I recently refinanced a loan for two clients, Susan and John. They had an unusual request: they asked me to calculate an interest rate with four points. The four points amounted to $23,000, which had to be added to the existing loan balance and amortized over thirty years. Susan and John wanted to lower their monthly payments and did not care how much equity was left on their property.

Points on refinancing loans can only be tax-deductible if the loan is used for home improvements. There is a great deal of tax-deduction information on the IRS website. In addition to reviewing that information, always consult a qualified tax preparer.

APR

APR, or annual percentage rate, is an official number created by the government as a standard to help consumers compare different loan programs. The APR has to appear on every interest rate advertisement aimed at the general public. An APR's calculation needs to include all the costs incurred during the process of obtaining a mortgage. It is based on the amortization period, such as thirty years.

An APR is supposed to be a true interest rate; in other words, it should be the cost of having a mortgage. Unfortunately, the way APR is calculated is both irrelevant and misleading in a real-world context. The majority of borrowers do not hold mortgages for thirty years. An APR also includes the cost of mortgage insurance, which many borrowers never have to pay, but it does not include title insurance premiums or the appraisal fee, which many borrowers do have to pay. In 2009, after thirty years of confusing borrowers, the Federal

Reserve proposed an amendment to TILA (Truth in Lending Act). We are still waiting for it in 2012.

Meanwhile, at the beginning of each loan transaction, lenders need to provide borrowers with Truth in Lending (TIL) information, which includes the APR. TIL is sent to borrowers along with the Good Faith Estimate (GFE) of the closing costs. Both documents are required by government regulations.

When our borrowers call us with a list of questions about these forms, utterly confused, I tell them not to pay much attention. By that point, they have already made major decisions about their loan, their interest rate, and the total costs. Those are the true numbers we thoroughly explained and the only ones they need to consider.

MORTGAGE INSURANCE

Mortgage insurance (MI) covers the risk that lenders take on when their borrowers offer a down payment of less than 20 percent. MI has existed since the FHA was created and is offered by insurance companies specializing in this field. Many borrowers call it *PMI*, which is actually the name of one of the insurance companies: Private Mortgage Insurance. Referring to mortgage insurance as PMI is like referring to facial tissue as Kleenex, or a photocopy as a Xerox. From 2008 and on, many MI companies suffered huge losses. Today, there are only a few that are still in business.

Mortgage insurance is paid in two ways: up-front and monthly fees. The amount of the fee depends on the loan's value. Between 2007 and 2011, mortgage insurance was tax-deductible. Since it can no longer be deducted, mortgage quotes are higher than they once were. **On April 9, 2012, mortgage insurance premiums for FHA loans went up.** The upfront fee increased from 1.0 percent to 1.75 percent of the loan amount. Annual renewal increases now depend on the LTV and the loan amount. While exact information is available on the FHA website, I recommend consulting an expert to find the right solution and combination of down payment and mortgage insurance costs.

Since FHA loan limits are higher than those of conventional loans—$729,750 instead of $625,000—those loans could be good alternatives even for the borrowers who can afford a down payment of 20 percent. Unfortunately, even in those cases, MI will be in place for five years unless the loan is amortized over fifteen years. In that case, MI would be waived.

IMPOUNDS

When lenders calculate a qualification for a loan, they use monthly mortgage payments plus prorated tax and home insurance figures. Property tax is paid twice a year, while insurance comes only once a year (unless there is a special arrangement). If a borrower puts less than 20 percent down, lenders might demand the creation of a special escrow or impound account, in which borrowers must place two months of the prorated insurance payments and a certain amount of the property tax payment. This amount is determined by the month in which escrow closes and can be equivalent to six months of payment.

In addition to this, remember there is going to be a monthly payment of both insurance and taxes. Therefore, buying with a small down payment can be quite costly. In contrast, it could be an attractive option for some borrowers, since finding money every time taxes and insurance are due can be challenging.

In our family, for example, we struggled with this issue for many years until we opened a separate account at our bank. We contributed money to that account every month, putting in amounts large enough to cover taxes and insurance (prorated monthly), along with some extra cash for house repairs. I suggest this simple technique to my clients, too.

If you choose or are obligated to have an impound account, I strongly recommend you monitor its monthly statements, especially if the mortgage is sold to another lender. Errors do happen and create unnecessary hassles. Impounds are also offered to borrowers who put 20 percent, or more, down for a reduction of a certain percentage of the mortgage's cost. When interest rates are quoted in the press or on the Internet, companies often use impounds to lower quoted rates.

LOAN ASSUMPTION

Sometimes borrowers ask if the mortgage is "assumable." So what does "assumable" mean? It's simple. There are cases in which an owner sells a property and the new owner simply takes over the previous owner's loan. In other words, the new owner "assumes" the previous owner's loan instead of getting a new one of his own.

Fixed-rate mortgages are not assumable, but adjustable mortgages can be. An assumption makes sense only if the old mortgage is more attractive than the best mortgage the purchaser could obtain in the current market. To assume a loan, new borrowers need to be qualified just as they would for a new loan, and the process might take even longer.

PREPAYMENT PENALTIES

Most of today's residential mortgages, especially fixed mortgages, do not have a prepayment penalty. In other words, a borrower is not penalized for paying off the balance of the loan before the term ends. You can pay off your thirty-year loan in twenty years, if you choose, but some adjustable-rate loan programs include a prepayment penalty, which can be hard or soft (waived in case of sale), and applied to either a refinance or the sale of property. This penalty can be set from one year to five and the amount can vary. In addition, a prepayment penalty can be "bought" in exchange for either a higher interest rate or points.

Most commercial loans have a prepay penalty that varies from lender to lender, set on a diminishing scale (5, 4, 3, 2, or 1 percent) for the whole fixed period, which is usually five years. Some programs allow the principal to be paid off by up to 20 percent per year without a prepayment penalty. Sometimes, when the interest rates drop, it is feasible to refinance, add the prepayment penalty to the new loan amount, and still lower your monthly payments.

BALLOON PAYMENTS

Balloon loans have almost disappeared from conventional residential loan scenarios. A balloon loan requires the borrower to pay the loan in full when the term of that loan expires. Balloon loans are loans that are not fully amortized. In other words, they are adjustable or non-fixed-rate loans.

Adjustable loans, which carry a fixed rate only briefly (for a period of, say, five to seven years), become adjustable after that fixed period. There is no balloon for those loans. The interest rate adjusts and the borrower goes on with his adjusted monthly payments.

Nevertheless, most commercial loans are balloon loans, since the majority of them are fixed for a short period of time. After the loan's expiration and the end of the prepay penalty period, the loan has to be paid off in full. This might present a challenge to those whose properties relied on rental income, which has diminished over time. Those borrowers would have a problem when they tried to qualify for a new loan. Fortunately, at Pacific Bay Financial, we have many creative solutions for such situations.

THE COST OF OBTAINING A MORTGAGE

This chapter addresses and answers some of the important questions borrowers ask (or should ask but forget) related to real money.

The first and most basic question is, "How much does it cost to get a mortgage, and who gets the money?" When you need the services of a doctor, an attorney, or any other professional provider, it is common knowledge that those professionals are paid for their time and level of expertise. However, the mortgage business works differently. Mortgage brokers are not paid until borrowers sign on the dotted line. Even then, we have to wait for three days in refinancing cases, giving borrowers the chance to change their minds or rescind the decision to take the loan.

Many circumstances can affect a mortgage broker's ability to get paid. It could be that a new credit report, which is ordered at the time of funding, shows a drop in the credit score because of a borrower's careless mistake. Then, the loan is cancelled. Alternatively, perhaps a loan is approved but the buyer changes his mind and decides not to go through with it after all. Perhaps the loan is approved but the borrower loses his job a week before the closing. Some borrowers who work with more than one mortgage company without disclosing this detail; obviously, only one company is going to be paid.

When clients wait for the rate to come down and their documents expire, we have to start the process all over again. In that case, we are doing twice the work for the same potential pay, essentially cutting our fees in half. Other obstacles can arise after we do most of the work: the appraiser may undervalue the property or a divorce process may cause a delay. All of these things affect our clients' ability to pay in a timely manner or, sometimes, at all.

When a transaction does not close, not only do we not get paid, but the title companies and banks do not get paid either. Even when the major banks decline 60 percent of loan applications, all those applications have to be processed and underwritten. There are a lot of participants involved in that work. However, the only players guaranteed payment, regardless of the outcome, are the credit report companies and the appraisers—even if their reports are worthless.

Despite all of this gloom and doom, at Pacific Bay Financial we are able to help a great deal of borrowers, and, at times, we earn lucrative fees. Fortunately for us, we close a significant number of loans despite any serious problems that may arise. When interest rates are low, we earn enough to pay off the debt we accumulate during the slow times, and we even manage to make some profit.

HOW BANKS CALCULATE THE RATES AND COSTS OF OFFERING MORTGAGES

Banks offer mortgages because the service is profitable. They make money from what's called the *spread* (that is, profit margins) and fees. Our compensation is part of the loan's price structure. In other words, our fee is included in the interest rate. Many banks have a special department, known as the secondary market desk, which calculates the price of each loan offer based on market fluctuations. Often the people in these departments have to bet on or hedge possible market changes. Depending on what the market does, the bank can earn or lose money rapidly.

When mortgage loans are sold, the profit margins are very slim. If the interest rate on a mortgage is 4 percent, for example, the lender needs to sell it at 3.5 percent to enjoy a profit of 0.5 percent. The more loans banks can close, the higher their profits are. To process more loans, they need more employees; however, hiring more employees eats into profits. If a bank does not have enough people, it takes longer to close loans and profits go down again. When a bank gets it right by suitably pricing loans and hiring good people to sell mortgages and close loans, profits rise.

MORTGAGE COSTS

When borrowers start the loan origination process, the lender or broker needs to run the client's credit report. Think of this process as similar to providing a doctor with an X-ray. Sometimes borrowers tell us they can provide us with a report that they can get for free. Unfortunately, free credit reports are not the kind we can use. They do not include credit scores, which are what lenders need. The type of credit report we use must have our company's name, be current, and include all three types of credit scores. Unfortunately, obtaining a credit score costs money. There is no way around it. All of this money goes to the credit company, which, in turn, pays all three credit repositories (the companies that calculate the scores).

When a loan process begins, a borrower has to fill out a credit card authorization form. This allows the lender to run a credit report and order an appraisal report. The credit report ordered by a mortgage broker or lender will cost you about $20. After all the necessary documents are collected, the loan package is sent to the lender electronically. After a few days and some procedural maneuverings, the appraisal is ordered. This comes at a cost of $450 or more. So, the potential borrower is already on the line for close to $500, which is a significant amount of money, without any guarantee he or she will get a satisfactory loan. These fees are not reimbursable or refundable for any reason.

In a similar leap of faith, the mortgage broker and the lender will spend a significant number of work hours without any guarantee they will earn even a penny.

WHAT IS ESCROW AND HOW DOES IT WORK?

At the beginning of a loan transaction, the loan processor opens what's called an *escrow*. If the loan transaction is a sales transaction, the real-estate agent opens an escrow. An escrow company is an organization that coordinates the flow of documents. On the East Coast, a real-estate attorney provides this service. The escrow company orders the *preliminary title report* (also know as a *prelim*), which is a document that describes the property and lists all liens, mortgages, taxes, and even alimony recorded against it. It's very important to work with an experienced escrow officer in order to ensure that the closing goes smoothly. Mistakes can be very costly and create a lot of headaches.

When an escrow company receives funds from a lender, the escrow company pays off all of the old mortgages and other loans, arranges the new mortgage's paperwork, notarizes the documents, and records the deed of trust (or mortgage) in the city or county recorder office.

Escrow companies are paid for both their escrow services and their title insurance services. (Title insurance guarantees both borrowers and lenders that the title is clean.) An escrow company's compensation is based on a combination of the loan amount and sale price. A handful of large escrow and title companies are regulated by the insurance commissioners, and their fees are comparable.

Lately, in the drive to save costs, title companies have let go of experienced, seasoned, and "expensive" employees, replacing them with lower-paid beginners. Since the success of our business depends on experience, we ensure we work with reliable escrow companies that have kept seasoned professionals on their payroll. **Some companies offer discounts, but it is risky to choose very sensitive services based on the price alone.** What the lower-priced companies do not tell you is that there can be additional fees for certain processing jobs. You get what you pay for.

One of my clients, Anna, called me from Seattle. She owned a property located in a rural area in Northern California, and she claimed to be free and clear (i.e., she had no loans). She wanted to increase her tenants' rent and pay off the tax lien, along with her credit card debts. In order to do all of this, she needed $350,000 to make improvements to her property. To find her the money, we had to define the transaction's character. Her income capacity was not enough to qualify for a conventional loan, her credit score was in the low 600s, and she had no savings capital. However, she had collateral. Her property could appraise for about $900,000. Besides, she owned another property: a two-unit building near San Francisco, which could be used as cross-collateral.

In a situation like this, there is only one solution: turning to a private lender who offers hard-money loans. However, when we received the *prelim, we were surprised to see a mortgage of $395,000. When I asked Anna about it, she told me that this loan had been paid off in 2010. It seemed that the payment was not reconvened back because of a breach in the chain of title. In other words, this transaction had not been properly recorded. Anna contacted her title company, which provided proof the loan had been paid off. We forwarded the proof to the title company and opened escrow. The mistake was corrected and a new prelim was issued, but all of this took a lot of time.*

PARTIES THAT MAKE MONEY DURING THE LOAN PROCESS

At the beginning of the loan process, the lender or mortgage broker prepares and sends a Good Faith Estimate (GFE) of the closing costs to the prospective borrower. A GFE is always accompanied by a Federal Truth in Lending Disclosure itemization of the amount financed. The document has to be signed and returned to the sender. The GFE contains the closing fees and other costs associated with the loan transaction (such as insurance, tax, transfer tax, and prorated interest-only payments for the previous loan and the new one).

Some years ago a GFE consisted of one page. It was a straight-forward document showing who gets paid, how much, and for what services. The mortgage broker's compensation was shown separately and usually amounted to 1 point of the loan amount plus a reasonable processing fee. This estimate was usually very close to the final amount, which appeared in the closing statement, also known as *HUD-1*. Then some government regulator added clauses to explain certain items and the GFE became a two-page document. Unfortunately, the matter did not stop there. More items were added and now a GFE is three pages long.

When the longer GFE was introduced, many lenders were scared: a small mistake, a single omission, or an unintentional under-calculation would require a lender to change the GFE and forward it to the borrower. If there were any mistakes or omissions, the lender and the broker would have to cover the costs. Now, in order to protect the lender, GFEs costs are usually overestimated. Lenders also hire specially trained people to double-check GFEs for errors. There can be changes during transactions, such as the reduction of the loan amount or increase of the interest rate. In those cases, new GFEs have to be recalculated and presented for borrower review and approval.

Borrowers are often confused by GFEs. It can seem as if there are too many fees and costs listed. Perhaps a borrower was told that closing costs would total about $3,500, but on the GFE they are listed at a much higher rate. In addition to the lender's and broker's compensations, closing costs include these basic items: an appraisal, credit reports, a notary, courier fees, title, escrow, and a flood certifi-cate (this is required to show the property is not located in a flood zone). What often confuses borrowers is the inclusion of other fees, such as insurance, property tax, transfer tax, and monthly payments for the previous mortgage (in cases of refinancing) and the new mortgage.

My wife and I have purchased homes in Las Vegas, most of which have been good investments, but there was a problem with one of them. We bought the property in September 2007, at the peak of the market, and were happy to overbid seven other buyers. According to the map we received, the house was located in a flood zone. We did not realize this when we bought the house. Even though the house turned out not to be in a flood zone, it took us a year to fix this problem. Meanwhile, we had to pay extra for flood insurance.

In hindsight, I should have canceled the transaction when I found out about the mapping error. Today, this property is really "under water," which, coincidentally, is a real-estate term that means the mortgage is higher than the value of the property.

Other closing costs can also creep in. If the property is a condominium, there might be a fee for the Homeowner's Association (HOA) certification or a *subordination fee*, which is charged on the second mortgage or the line of credit. However, this subordination fee, like the fee for the appraisal and the credit report, is paid during the loan process. The closing costs include fees, such as the underwriting fee, collected by the lender. Mortgage brokers are not allowed to collect processing fees any longer. All of these fees are combined to create closing costs.

NO OUT-OF-POCKET CLOSING COST LOANS

In cases in which a borrower chooses a loan with "no closing costs," which actually means no *out-of-pocket* closing costs (since closing costs never really go away), the lender needs to offer the borrower a rebate, which is offset by the higher interest rate. The rebate must be large enough to cover the closing costs. When borrowers "shop" for a rate, it can be the same or different. What will change is the rebate. Higher rates will have higher rebates and vice versa. The objective is to be sure the rebate amount is enough to cover the total closing costs. If it is not, the difference is added to the existing loan amount. If borrowers choose to have a lower rate, they have to be ready to pay the closing costs as well as points.

For example, one day the rate could be 4 percent with a rebate of $3,578. This might be enough to offer a no-closing-costs rate. The next day the rate might be the same, 4 percent, but the market could worsen. In that case, the rebate would only add up to $2,632. This means the rebate would not cover about $1,000 of the closing costs. Instead, this amount could be added to the loan or paid out of the borrower's pocket. If the borrower became concerned the rate might go higher, he or she could lock in the rate and the cost. This process, known as "floating" the rate, locks in a future date when rates or rebates could decrease again.

Since we usually lock in rates when the file is ready to go to the lender, it is difficult to take advantage of any last-minute rate change. I compare this process to that of buying corporate stocks. After a stockbroker has executed his transaction, the exchange is done until the next change in price. Similarly, when interest rates drop, as they have recently, and a client chooses a "no-cost loan," we can refinance again after 150 to 180 days, depending on the lender. If the refinancing is done before the lender's wait period ends, the loan originator has to reimburse the lender for the amount of fees received.

During refinancing, the existing loan's balance is paid off as of the first of the month. This leaves the interest rate to be paid during the new month's remaining days. For example, if the transaction closes in the middle of the month, the previous lender **is paid the prorated interest** only prior to the date of the closing. The new lender **is also paid** a prorated amount for the remaining days in the month and the new, full payment starts a month later. If the transaction closes in the middle of February, for example, the first payment in full will be due April 1.

In the purchase transaction, closing costs are higher because of title and escrow fees, which are based on the sale price. There might also be pest report and contractor inspection fees, as well as septic inspections, or any number of inspections specific to the property in question. The previous owner has to be reimbursed for the prepaid property taxes. At the same time, non-recurring and closing costs can be negotiated to be paid by the seller or the buyer in a so-called buyer's market. Usually, when deficiencies are found during an inspection, instead of reimbursing the buyer for the repairs, real-estate agents subsidize the amount and the buyer pays non-recurring closing costs, which are limited to 6 percent and depend on the LTV.

OUR COMPANY, PACIFIC BAY FINANCIAL

I n 1983, when I started in the mortgage business, it was like the Wild West. My office was located in San Ramon, a forty-five-minute drive from San Francisco, and all of the surrounding areas were just barren hills. Now, these hills are all filled with new buildings. Mortgage interest rates were around 15 percent back then, and sales prices and loan amounts were relatively low. The company I joined, Colwell Financial, was a mortgage bank, and we had a very limited, fixed-rate loan program to sell. The predominant sources for mortgages were savings and loans banks, which offered adjustable loans. We were told that one of them, Home Savings, used a "mirror test" as its underwriting guidance. As long as the borrower could fog a mirror with his breath, he was qualified.

My break came when Colwell Financial signed a correspondent agreement with World Savings and Loan. Suddenly I had a product to sell. I went back and forth from San Francisco to San Ramon, delivering my loan packages, and I quickly became the company's top producer. After nine months we realized that driving slowed me down, so I requested an office in San Francisco. First, I conducted my business from the storage room by our garage. Just a month later I rented a tiny space of my own, which had been a broom closet in a local real-estate office.

What I did next seemed to make no sense. After graduating from the Louis Salinger Academy of Fashion, my wife, Elfa, had been working as a fashion designer, fulfilling her childhood dream. One day I told her I wanted her to go to night school so she could earn a real-estate license and help me in the mortgage business. She could have said no, but she didn't. Somehow, after being married to me for seventeen years and having followed along with my other "crazy" ideas, she knew this was going to be all right. We still work together and have been happily married for more than forty-five years.

With Elfa at my side, my business grew through referrals, primarily from real-estate offices, where I conducted educational classes on mortgage lending. One small real-estate company, which was owned by two partners, referred a lot of business to me. One day they told me they would like to start their own mortgage company, and they invited me to join them. My wife was against it, but I was afraid to lose business, so I said yes. By that time, I had been in the mortgage business for one year. We had closed many loans and earned decent money.

Nine months later, I changed my mind and agreed with my wife. We dissolved the partnership. In September 1985, Elfa and I started our own company, Pacific Bay Financial Corporation, which became known as a leading (and is now the oldest surviving) mortgage brokerage firm in the Bay Area.

Somewhere between 1985 and today the mortgage business became the mortgage industry. Interest rates came down. Savings and loans prospered and then disappeared. Thanks to the evolution of mortgage-based securities, mortgage banks and firms grew like mushrooms after the rain. This growth, in turn, triggered a tremendous explosion of additional growth among mortgage brokerage firms. Non-regulated Wall Street firms had a ball in the secondary market, which is where mortgage-backed securities were sold. These firms made enormous profits, inventing more and more "creative products" that were peddled through commercial and mortgage banks and sold by mortgage brokers.

We all experienced ups and downs. Some years we made a lot of money; in other years, we basically went from feast to famine. Sometimes we didn't have enough to pay the rent or pay ourselves. Yet somehow we managed to pay our employees, and they loyally stayed with us through the years. Recently, one of our first employees retired after working for us for more than twenty-five years.

At Pacific Bay, we also developed an unusual way of doing business. Whereas other mortgage companies typically hired a bunch of agents who had to find their own business deals and processed their own loans, we employed high-producing loan consultants and paired each of them up with a dedicated underwriter.

This practice put a burden on our company's bottom line. Perhaps it was not the best fiscal decision. Nevertheless, we still employ many of the same people who, like the proverbial prolific bunnies, continue originating loans, primarily from the same client base. The last three years have been tough for our company, just like they have been for many other companies. Luckily, from a personal standpoint, the mortgage payments on our house are low. As time passed, Elfa and I took out a business line of credit. When this was no longer enough, we borrowed more and invested our own money. The end of 2010 finally brought relief for us, along with many others. Interest rates dropped and we were able to refinance loans for a good number of our clients.

However, in January 2011 the volume dropped again. In July 2011 we originated only twenty-seven loans and closed twenty-nine. We need fifty to break even. All of our resources had dried up. Finally, a miracle happened. In August of that year, our loan origination count reached 142. It was an avalanche: we could barely handle the volume. We even broke our own rule and allowed some employees to work a few hours of overtime.

Unfortunately, banks could not handle the volume in a timely manner. Some ran out of money and could not issue loans. At the same time, the jumbo-conforming-loan limit was lowered from $727,750 to $625,500. This bad timing put additional pressure on everyone. Still, rates remained low over the next few months, and we continued to help many borrowers lower their monthly payments.

During all these years, my focus has been on originating loans, working with clients, motivating and educating our loan agents, developing relationships with new mortgage sources, and making sure our company doors have stayed open. My wife has had the more difficult task. She has been in charge of administration and finances. Whenever there has been a shortage, she has been placed under significant emotional pressure. She can also be the cold shower to my great ideas. After years of working and living together, I have learned to trust her intuition. In all the time we have been together, I have never made and would never make any decision, especially one about people, without her consent.

For example, she approved the decision I made several years ago to open another office in San Francisco. At this office, we started a commercial department, which led to the creation of a separate company that focuses on originating commercial loans. The commercial field is as open today as the residential brokerage field was thirty years ago.

Our success has helped us meet a string of continuous challenges. In April 2011, for example, the Federal Reserve Bank created conditions that threatened our ability to stay in the business as mortgage brokers. Initially, I had no idea which direction to go. However, where there is a will, there is a way. We decided to join a dynamic and growing local mortgage bank, Bay Equity. Our decision will help us continue to provide our services to our valuable clients, people who have stayed loyal to us throughout the years. As a consequence of this initial decision, and a means of strengthening our company, we divided our agents into two groups. Those who specialized in residential loans became employees of Bay Equity. Pacific Bay Financial officially became a commercial mortgage broker, although this branch of our company still helps clients with their residential loans.

THE IMPORTANCE OF A MORTGAGE BROKER

Over the last thirty years, mortgage brokers multiplied from a few to many thousands. Then, in 2008, mortgage banks that depended on lines of credit started dropping like flies. Along with them went mortgage brokerage companies. At the peak of the mortgage boom, mortgage brokers had originated more than 50 percent of all loans; then, almost overnight, they were gone. Significantly, the banks, which, together with Wall Street, had allowed rotten mortgage products to reach the market, were blaming mortgage brokers for all of the subprime meltdown's ills. Major banks cut their relationships with remaining mortgage brokers: for example, Citibank reduced its number of approved brokers from 9,000 to 1,000. Pacific Bay was among the privileged ones that remained. Then, however, Citibank pulled out of the wholesale mortgage business altogether. After the acquisition fiasco with Countrywide, Bank of America also eliminated its connections with mortgage brokers. So did Chase, then MetLife, then ING, and, most recently, Wells Fargo. Many smaller banks still work with mortgage brokers and, of course, some mortgage banks sell their loans strictly through mortgage brokerage channels.

To control "unruly" mortgage brokers, at least the few who were left, the government set up a universal registry. To become registered, everyone involved in loan origination, excluding banks, had to pass two tests, complete an additional eight hours per year of education, report every month's production, and, of course, pay an extra fee to a specially created agency. I suspect all this was part of the government's plans to create "new jobs" after thousands of self-employed, hard-working women and men lost theirs.

In the past, mortgage brokers earned their fees in relation to each loan's wholesale price, which was either one point or one percent less than retail. When we needed to explain our compensation to clients, we compared our compensation method to the way travel agents are paid.

If, on the same day, a borrower inquired about a mortgage at a bank and at a mortgage broker's, our quotes would be identical. Banks would pay the brokers the required point at the close of escrow. This did not change the rate and everyone was satisfied. To cover additional services and expenses, brokers would charge a processing fee (similar to what banks charge as extra fees). While a few unscrupulous brokers tried to collect more than their share, there was stiff competition. Sometimes, we had to lower our compensation just to make things work.

Everything changed on April 1, 2011. At that point, the government decided to control how much we brokers would be allowed to earn. There would be no more processing fees for mortgage brokers. Set compensation had to be fixed for ninety days. At first, these changes created a lot of confusion, since the new rules did not apply to banks. California was one of the few states that showed pioneer spirit and allowed mortgage brokers to remain self-employed.

When we at Pacific Bay joined Bay Equity, most of our independent agents became employees, which increased our company's overall costs by about 15 percent. As a mortgage bank, we can collect a processing fee and charge more than a point to cover extra costs. Because of the shift in underwriting guidance, our workload and costs increased significantly. Yet we are still in business.

In the end, the borrowers are paying extra for the elimination of competition and unnecessary government intervention. Today, when only a few huge banks are trying to run the mortgage show, offering limited products and even more limited solutions, the role of the mortgage broker, whose business is to find solutions among various sources, becomes even more valuable than ever before. Unfortunately, it is tough to survive in such an environment, and it seems that the big banks and the government are trying to get rid of small "competitors."

This scenario calls to mind the story of the rabbit and the fox. One day, when Papa Rabbit was away in the cabbage field and Mama Rabbit was busy preparing food, the fox came and ate all of the baby rabbits. When Papa Rabbit came home and found out what happened, he began to beat Mama Rabbit. A friend asked him, "Why are you doing that?"

"Well," said Papa Rabbit, "I cannot beat the fox."

In spite of all these challenges, the share of loans originated by mortgage brokers has grown. In the first quarter of 2012, brokers captured 11.4 percent of loans, according to the publication *Origination News*. This number will continue to grow, since banks cannot offer choices and solutions the way brokers can.

WHAT MORTGAGE BROKERS DO

When we joined the Bay Equity mortgage bank, one of our conditions was that we should be able to broker loans through other lenders. Currently, we work with close to thirty mortgage companies. Thus, while acting as mortgage *bankers*, which gives us some control over the underwriting process, we can still offer mortgage *broker* services.

Many borrowers who apply for loans have difficulty comprehending what mortgage brokers actually do. To become a professional mortgage broker, one needs to learn how to think. At least, that has been our company philosophy. Unlike banks, we do not sell mortgages. Instead, we look for solutions. We need to use many different banks and their different mortgage products to retain the necessary variations of underwriting guidance and diversity. This is the best way to help our clients. While obtaining a low interest rate is an important goal, there are other considerations at work too.

A young doctor wanted to buy his first home. He had his heart set on a condominium that cost more than $960,000. He had a down payment of 10 percent and his employers at the hospital, where he earned a very good salary, offered to match that with another 10 percent. Major banks had used to honor this type of arrangement, but had recently stopped doing so. Fortunately, we found one local bank that was familiar with these programs and was comfortable working with them. However, *since the amount of the mortgage was jumbo, the bank did not have a thirty-year fixed rate. Instead, the bank offered a five-year fixed loan.*

Since our client did not have any experience with mortgages, he was concerned about what would happen five years later, when his loan would adjust. I had to explain possible scenarios and also find a way to make him comfortable with this choice if, indeed, it was his only option.

Because we are so deeply involved with our clients during the loan process, many of them become our friends and many of them come back to us, even twenty years later. What amazes me is that I always remember both the circumstances of their loans and their interest rates. One side of my business card states, "Only for referral." The other side states, "We invest 100 percent of our time delivering first-class service to our clients. As a result, our valuable customers, suppliers, and friends refer their family members, co workers, neighbors, and other people they know to ask for advice on getting a loan or buying real estate. We are interested in building strong, life-long relationships, one person at a time." It is an honor to be a mortgage broker.

E I G H T

CHANGES IN THE LENDING INDUSTRY

I recently had a conversation with a residential mortgage originator who has been in the business for a while. He complained again and again. "I cannot stand it any more," he said. "I submitted a loan package to a lender at Thanksgiving and it is only now closing in February. They were asking for ridiculous stuff, like, 'Why is the address on the pay stub different?' While they were underwriting, some documents passed the two-month mark and new ones needed to be provided. And then, at the time of closing, the lender asked where the $500 to pay for the closing costs came from."

For many years before the economic meltdown, lenders who offered stated-income or stated-asset loans barely asked for anything. A borrower or broker just needed a handwritten loan application that listed any kind of "creative" assets and income, a preliminary title report, and an appraisal report. That was it.

This reminds me of a story about a company that was looking to hire an accountant. The interviewer asked every applicant the same question: "How much is two times two?"

The first applicant answered, "Four."

The second answered, "Three."

The third one asked, "How much do you need?"

Guess which one was hired.

At the time of subprime and stated income loans, everybody and their brothers became mortgage brokers. Real estate was booming. This was good news for the economy and the politicians who did not give a damn what Wall Street or the big banks were doing.

This brings to mind another story I heard. This allegedly took place in Shanghai during World War II. At that point in time, Shanghai was one of the few places in the world that welcomed Jewish refugees who fled from Nazi-infested Eastern Europe.

Since immigrants could not do much upon their arrival, many became engaged in trading boxes of sardines. One would sell to another and make a few pennies, and so on. This continued until one of the buyers opened a box and realized there were no sardines in it. He brought the box back and angrily complained that he had been cheated. "You idiot," the seller answered. "You have to sell the box, not open it."

Unfortunately, this metaphoric transaction happened in other places besides Shanghai. It happened in the United States. Sooner or later, that "box" was going to be opened. First, we had the Enron affair, which was based on "empty boxes" and double accounting. This was a prelude to the end of the company's "good times." More boxes on Wall Street, which were called *derivatives* and other fancy names, started to pop up. All this led to the collapse of the whole financial infrastructure in the United States and in any country in Europe that had bought "empty boxes" from us.

Huge financial institutions, like AIG and the more than 100-year-old Solomon Brothers, were the first to fall. Other Wall Street companies and too-big-to-fail banks, which had to be rescued by the government, followed.

Then a remarkable thing happened. Someone had to be blamed. It was easy. The finger pointed at the mortgage brokers. Regardless of who really was at fault, life continued. As some say, the loan-underwriting pendulum swung in new directions. The government had to rescue Fannie Mae and Freddie Mac, which had sustained huge losses because borrowers had stopped paying their mortgages. The secondary market, where all of the wheeling and dealing took place, disappeared. With it, so did choices and mortgage solutions for many homeowners.

What is happening now in the mortgage business is a return to the basics: the Five Cs. This means underwriting guidance has to be followed and enforced. Some guidance might not make sense on the surface; borrowers sometimes get upset when they hear about more and more conditions they have to meet throughout the process. We often hear the question—asked in an understandably irritable tone—"Couldn't they ask for everything at once?" The answer, unfortunately, is always no. That's because after the underwriter receives and reviews documents, he or she might notice inconsistencies (such as a "different address on the pay stub"). Those inconsistencies need to be dealt with and explained.

Paul wanted to refinance his mortgage to lower his monthly payments. He was a self-employed contractor, but he was paying himself a monthly salary and he had pay stubs to prove it. In 2011, business was good. He was able to increase his salary significantly. If he had been a self-employed contractor who had left his business to work for another company as an employee, a lender would have considered his salary without question. However, Paul remained self-employed.

From an underwriting point of view, the only way to calculate Paul's income was to average it over the previous two years. Paul had a problem, since Paul's 2011 tax returns would take a while to be prepared. To resolve the problem, I took his file and a 2011 W-2 form to the underwriter at our mortgage bank. Since Paul had a low LTV, good credit, and strong cash reserves, his loan was approved.

Face-to-face underwriting is not common practice. Usually a loan scenario is e-mailed to various banks, one at a time, for review. After this, the lender is chosen, based on the company's conditions and the interest rate offered. After our processor collects all of the documents, the file is electronically forwarded to the lending company of our choice. This company might have the best rate or be able to approve the loan regardless of the rate or type of program. For us, the rate determines the mortgage payment, which is a factor in the borrower's ability to qualify. Despite our best efforts, not every loan is approved. The appraised value is often one of the major problems over which we have little control.

"Many People Apply for Loans but Few Can Qualify." This was the headline on an article in a San Francisco-area newspaper in late 2011. The article pointed out that in spite of historically low interest rates, banks had turned down many borrowers. This was sad but true. Our company employs two associates who are former loan originators from one of the big banks, and they both told me the bank approves only 40 percent of its loan applications.

Because we pre-underwrite loan applications—that is, we analyze every file before starting to work on it—less than 10 percent of our applications are declined. Borrowers may lack just one or two things (in any of the Five Cs). Sometimes it only takes a little time to find a solution when it comes to capacity (that is, how income is reported and calculated). At other times we have to wait for the new tax returns to be completed, and then wait a few more months before the IRS accepts them. When it comes to improving a credit score, a borrower may have to find, say, $21,000 to pay down balances on eight credit cards in order to increase his score to 700. We may also have to find ways to show reserves. For example, a client came to us after her loan had been turned down because her down payment came from her business account. We showed her that her IRA account could be used instead, and we got her loan approved. When it comes to character, we may have to find a lender that has creative ways of dealing with specific circumstances.

Sometimes, we come up against the issue of collateral, the most challenging hurdle of the Cs and the basis of the lending industry. Strategies for addressing collateral problems are discussed in the next section.

THE VALUE OF APPRAISAL REPORTS

As I have mentioned before, the portion of collateral based on the value of a building is determined by an appraisal report. Lenders use an LTV ratio to determine how much collateral an applicant might have, which in turn establishes the level of risk the lender would assume. From there, the lender can establish criteria, including the interest rate, the loan amount, the loan terms, and the applicant's ability to earn income from the property (through renting, for example).

An appraisal report is prepared by a person who has specific knowledge, years of training, and familiarity with the area in which they specialize. At least, this is how it used to be. On May 4, 2009, in the midst of turmoil across the lending industry, the government introduced a new law called the Home Valuation Code of Conduct (HVCC).

Before this change, appraisers worked as individuals or joined small companies. Their standard fee was between $300 and $350, and they charged a higher fee for bigger or more complex properties. They could appraise two to three properties a day and still produce good reports.

Brokers could call them and discuss property value before spending clients' money. If there happened to be a rush, an appraiser would speed up the process and get the results sooner. If they found something detrimental in an inspection, such as peeling paint or water-stained ceilings, they would inform us, and we would encourage the client to fix it before an official appraisal report was completed.

We never interfered with appraisal work or demanded an appraiser change the value of a property. After all, each appraiser provided an opinion dependent on the market conditions of the day, along with their skills and expertise.

Today, in contrast, to order an appraisal report, a client needs to give the lender a credit card number. This number is charged even if there is not enough equity in the property to get a mortgage. In that case, the appraisal report and the client's money are both wasted. Moreover, since the appraisal report is ordered only after the borrower receives the GFE (that is, after a major part of our work is done), not only do we not get paid, but we also have to upset our client. (After that, it is unlikely the client will refer our services to his friends.) After we put the loan file together, we send it electronically to the lender, who in turn will send a request to an appraisal management company (AMC). Major banks often own AMCs, which are formed like cooperatives. The appraisal fee has increased to an average of $450. About $200 of that fee is paid to the appraiser, while the rest is divided between the AMC and its owner.

Because reports are ordered randomly from an "available appraiser," in some instances, an appraiser from Sacramento might do a report in San Francisco. In cases such as these, the results are devastating. To make a living, appraisers have to work fast. Thus, they can make many mistakes. They may use the wrong comparative homes and often report values that are less than what is needed to qualify for a loan. However, no one involved in the loan process is allowed to communicate with the appraiser, so the whole thing comes down to a hold-your-breath-and-cross-your-fingers situation.

Disputes can occur after the fact and values can be corrected sometimes, but all this delays the process. A delay can result in the loss of an interest rate or even the sale itself. Sometimes we have to go to different lenders to obtain different results; then, the client has to pay yet another appraisal fee without any guarantee that things will work out. In one recent case, we hired an independent appraiser who wrote comments indicating mistakes made by the AMC appraiser and calculated a higher value. While the bank accepted the report, it decided not to grant the mortgage.

After an appraisal report is completed, the lender typically forwards it to another appraisal firm whose job is to check the report for errors. This is important because if errors are found in the documents after the loan is sold to Fannie Mae or Freddie Mac, the loan has to be repurchased (sent back to the lender). Since there are no other buyers at that point, the lenders are stuck. They cannot use their line of credit to generate new loans, so they are extra cautious—bordering on paranoid—in the underwriting process, especially when it comes to "unnecessary conditions." All of this, of course, delays the real-estate market's recovery, which is currently rife with overkill.

This brings to mind a story I heard when I was quite young. When I was in the fourth grade, I had a teacher who had taught in China for many years. She told us that in China, a teacher would leave the classroom in the middle of a test and no one would cheat.

She also told us that one day the Chinese government decided to get rid of all the flies. They gave their one billion citizens flyswatters. Soon the flies were gone. Yet the government did not realize the potential consequences of its actions: the particular birds that ate the flies started to die too. Since these birds were part of the forest ecology, the trees became sick and the chain reaction continued, resulting in widespread trouble. This is what is happening today in the United States' real-estate industry.

WHAT LIES AHEAD: HOW WE CAN TAKE ADVANTAGE OF CURRENT MARKET SITUATIONS

Throughout my career, I have been reminded of the proverb, "Seek for seeds of victory in every defeat." When the mortgage industry started to tumble and our business and income slowed down, I said to myself, "This situation was created especially for me. What can I learn? What can I do differently? How can I help my clients?" With

God's help, we have somehow survived. Now, when interest rates are incredibly low, we are able to help many of our clients.

More and more frequently, people—especially young people—are taking advantage of the drop in real-estate values to buy their first homes. Some people have been buying foreclosed properties for 10 to 50 cents on the dollar. Some people put together funds and scout the country for the best bargains. The trick, in each case, is obtaining financing, since most residential lenders can only finance up to four properties for one borrower, while other lenders can finance up to ten properties per borrower. To qualify for non-owner-occupied loans, borrowers need to show reserves equaling six months of mortgage payments plus taxes and insurance for each property they own. Not too many people can do this.

When investors buy foreclosed properties, they make repairs. Then, they either rent and pray for future appreciation, or sell to qualified buyers. Often, they use FHA loans. Those who are able to avoid foreclosure by selling property through short sales, can preserve their credit rating. After two to three years, such a person can buy another property for less than the amount for which he or she sold the previous property. (This tactic is preferable to submitting to foreclosure, since it takes seven years to erase a foreclosure from a credit report.)

This scenario reminds me of a story about a boy who came home from school and complained to his father about the horrible thing that had happened to him that day. The father asked, "Do you remember a horrible thing that happened to you a year ago?"

"No," the boy answered.

"A year from today, you will not remember this one either," his father concluded.

No one can predict the future, and most of us have short memories. Still, I have a crystal ball on my desk. It is actually a very heavy glass ball, but it looks the part. When clients ask me if the market will improve, I direct them to my crystal ball and offer them self-service.

THE BENEFITS OF BUYING REAL ESTATE

To buy, or not to buy: that is the question. While I'm sure Shakespeare was not concerned about this question when he wrote *Hamlet*, many of us are concerned about it today. When I was growing up in Riga, Latvia, a Soviet strategy surrounded many consumer products, including cars. Owning a car was not only a privilege; it was also a liability. As difficult as it was to buy a car, it was even more difficult to maintain and repair one.

One of my very first jobs was as a mechanic at a garage that serviced trucks. Whenever a new truck arrived, I was supposed to have the necessary tools in my toolbox, but usually the toolbox was empty. We would weld our old tools in order to preserve them, and since new ones were not available, I kept my best wrench attached to my belt with a chain. People in Latvia said that a car owner had two joys in his life: the day he bought his car and the day he got rid of it.

Millions of American homeowners today wish they had never bought property. Recently, state attorneys and the five major banks reached settlements worth $26 billion to compensate some of the homeowners who had suffered from our economy's collapse. I purposely did not write "the collapse of the real-estate market" in that last sentence, though there is an estimate that the value of real estate dropped by $7 trillion between the 2006 real-estate bubble and the beginning of 2012.

There is a saying these days: "It's the economy, stupid." Sure it is. It seems many smart people, including leading economists, could not predict the obvious: if you build a castle on the sand, sooner or later there will be no castle. Perhaps the politicians who are supposed to lead us, but who usually react after the fact, just did not know or care how to do it right.

So, why buy real estate? There are at least three reasons to buy property. First, you own your home. You build equity and don't just throw money down the tubes on rent. Second, real estate usually appreciates over time and becomes an investment alternative to stocks and bonds. Third, when you own real estate, you are afforded a tax deduction. While this last point is not a very good reason to buy real estate on its own, it is an added bonus.

When my family moved to San Francisco, we spent a few days living in that inexpensive hotel on Leavenworth Street where we saw prostitutes and pimps from our window every day. Soon after, we were lucky to find an apartment in a two-story building. All five of our family members slept in a two-bedroom apartment. The owners were a Chinese couple who lived in the unit downstairs.

When our landlady cooked, she would open all of the doors and windows, and the aroma would fill our small apartment. Trust me—the aroma was not good. However, our children's school was nearby and Golden Gate Park was only a few blocks away. Plus, despite having a cramped, sometimes stinky apartment, we lived in what we believed to be the best city in the world. After a while, by the time I had started working again and we had sold our house in Israel, we suddenly became "rich"—or, at least, rich by comparison. We moved out of the apartment and rented a house. We lived in this rental until we bought our home in 1984.

When we bought this property, we had very little money, question-able income possibilities, and a five-member family. Our actions did not make much sense. However, I think we acted on the same reasoning that many people use when they make decisions that, on the surface, do not appear to make any sense. It is simple. As human beings, most of us have a drive to better our lives: to create better conditions for our children. This, of course, was one of the strongest motivating factors that had uprooted millions of families and drawn immigrants to the Land of Opportunity. I knew that was my motivation, too.

I think all people are optimists by nature and believe everything is going to be all right. At the same time, I have learned that owning a home is not for everyone. Owning real estate is both a responsibility and a huge liability. As my late mother-in-law used to say, "It is better to be a rich tenant than a poor homeowner." When my wife and I bought a rental property years ago, I was concerned my tenants would move out and I would have to struggle to pay the mortgage with my own money. Renters do move out eventually, and guess who has to cover that monthly payment while new tenants are found? The person who received the mortgage for the property. It does not matter to the lender if the property is vacant. The lender just wants to receive a monthly payment on time. Everyone knows what happens when this doesn't happen.

At one point, when my wife and I owned a four-unit apartment building in San Francisco, the roof began to leak, and we had no money to repair it. We also had an adjustable mortgage that had started at 9 percent interest, gone up to 10 percent, and then hit 11 percent—and we could not refinance it. This situation reminds me of the old saying, "The cobbler's children do not have shoes."

I'm thankful that none of my tenants have had this problem. We made sure to fix our home when needed, always finding the money somehow. When you own property, you build equity, whether it is your money or someone else's money covering the mortgage payments. This is the first of the reasons to consider buying real estate, as mentioned earlier.

Once again, another reason to buy real estate is that the property will appreciate over time. Its value will increase; eventually, it could be worth substantially more than the purchase price. Of course, the overall appreciation depends on when you bought the real estate and for how long you owned it. According to the U.S. Census, the value of new homes purchased from 1963 to 2008 increased by 5.4 percent. The National Association of Realtors finds the same percentage in their study, which includes the years 1968 to 2009. Since this rate is an average, and since eventually new homes become old ones requiring upkeep and maintenance, the figure is probably closer to 4 percent. Four percent is about the same as the rate of inflation. This means that the value of money is the same.

What has happened in recent years has been the opposite of appreciation: *depreciation*. For example, according to DataQuick. com, median Bay Area residential prices peaked in the middle of

2007, at $665,000. In January 2012, the number was $351,000. In other words, people who bought real estate in 2007 lost a bundle. People who buy now, or in the immediate future, might see values start to climb again. However, the question remains: is purchasing worth it? Median prices could go down even more.

Why not to continue to rent, then? Websites galore offer buy-versus-rent calculators. These should be used as brain exercises or to satisfy curiosity; in my opinion, which has been formed over many years of experience, people buy when they are ready. It's as simple as that.

Purchasing real estate provides the buyer with a home, but the purchase also acts as an investment: buying a house is a legitimate alternative to purchasing stocks and bonds or other financial products. Investing in stocks requires expertise that most of us do not have. The stock market seems like it's full of numbers and theories floating out in space. In contrast, a house is a tangible commodity.

Besides, purchasing a house can also help lower the owner's taxes, albeit on a small scale. Some borrowers come to me and say, "I'm tired of making my landlord rich, and I'm tired of giving so much to Uncle Sam in taxes." While it's true that mortgage payments can be deductions, only the interest portion is actually deductible. Even then, the amount that can be deducted is determined by the individual's tax bracket. **A certain percentage of property taxes is also deductible.** Bear in mind, though, that the cost of home ownership can outweigh all tax benefits. Remember, it is never a good idea to purchase real estate based on the tax deduction alone.

So, when is it a good time to purchase real estate? If you are married, the best time would be when your wife tells you so. I am only half-joking. In my opinion, among most home-buying couples, decisions are made by the woman. Often, the decisions are based on emotion, rather than on logic or calculation. In my opinion, a woman's intuition is usually accurate. In my experience, a woman generally knows if a house is the right house for her family. If you are not married, you should consult with someone who has good intuition, or you could just trust your own judgment.

Emotions aside, sometimes the economy plays tricks on us. How about those who bought homes in 2007, or even earlier? Consider the statistics mentioned earlier. Obviously, up through 2009, buyers continued to buy even when the market was bad. Between 2004 and 2007, the majority of real-estate purchases were made by borrowers who received their mortgages in *violation* of the Five Cs. Stated asset loans gave license for borrowers to lie. People who had low credit scores, no down payment, and no income received mortgages. What could be more insane? On top of that, those same people were offered second loans and lines of credit with no consideration about their equity or how they might repay the loans.

I cannot claim innocence myself. We were in this type of situation when we bought our house in 1984. Like anyone else who was in the mortgage business in those "good" years, my wife and I had a ball and benefited financially from the banks' shortsighted-ness. However, as a Russian saying goes, "The lie has short legs and sooner or later the game will come to an end." During those years of subprime lending I wanted to write a book about the situation. I planned to title it *There Is No Truth in Lending*, a play on the name of the document sent to most borrowers, the TIL (Truth in Lending). In hindsight, I do not think anyone would have bought a book with that title at the time. Besides, I was too busy accommodating anxious borrowers to focus on a book project.

All this reminds me of a story about a man who traveled the world in search of the truth. He went from country to country asking people if they knew where the truth lived. No one knew. Finally, the traveler came upon an old monk in the Himalayas. The monk said he thought the truth lived in a cave at the very top of a mountain. So, the man climbed the mountain and eventually came upon a cave. There he found an ugly, toothless old woman.

"I'm looking for the truth," the man said.

"I am the truth," the woman answered. "And you are welcome to stay with me to learn more about the truth."

Years passed. One day, the woman said to the man, "Now you know everything I know. Go to the people and spread the word about the truth."

The man bowed to her and agreed.

When he was ready to depart, she said, "Can I ask you for a big favor?"

"Of course," the man responded.

"Can you tell the world," the woman said, "that I am young and beautiful?"

Will appreciation of property come back? Sure. In 1994 and 1995, we also saw a slump in real estate. One difference between then and now is that back then the government did not try to help, and the market corrected itself. I remember bankers being surprised that borrowers continued to pay their mortgages in spite of the drop in value. Of course, the other major difference is that back then people still had their jobs.

WHEN TO REFINANCE AND WHY

The obvious answer to the question of when to refinance is to move when interest rates decrease. While homeowners can lower their monthly payments through refinancing, what about the cost of the refinancing itself? Again, the obvious answer is that refinancing has to be feasible. In spite of the fact that this process seems simple and many borrowers refinance, many others do not.

Let's take a look at a typical scenario. In 2011, when interest rates dropped a considerable amount, two borrowers (a married couple) were lucky; they were able to refinance and obtain a thirty-year, fixed-rate loan at 4.5 percent. They had monthly payments of about $2,386 to meet the conforming-limit loan (which was about $417,000) for their single-family property, and they had about $3,500 in closing costs. Was this worth doing?

To answer, let's check in with an old rule that is heavily promoted in mortgage books and the press. According to this rule, it is only feasible to refinance when the rate drops 2 percent. (I'm not sure where this 2 percent came from.) In this case, the rate would have to be 2.5 percent in order for the family to refinance again.

Today, interest rates have dropped significantly, and there is confusion about finding the number at which refinancing makes sense. Those who check the Web or receive advertisements in the mail can see rates as low as 3.5 percent that are fixed for thirty years. Yet how much will it cost to obtain such a rate? It is feasible to pay closing costs and perhaps points, but not too many. Even more important is the question of whether the borrower will be qualified to receive such a rate. Many changes can happen in any of the Cs over a year's time.

Most borrowers whom we refinanced in the summer of 2012 had loans of up to $417,000 and received a typical rate of 3.875 percent with no **out-of-pocket closing costs**. This lowered the monthly payments on a $417,000 loan to about $1,961. If the interest rate is lower, the savings can be greater still. However, this savings could require paying the closing costs and/or points, which can take a number of years to recover.

While the benefits might be obvious, some borrowers delay refinancing. The main reason is that people do not like to deal with paperwork and rely on lenders' mercy. I know the feeling. When it comes time to doing our own refinancing, I am an expert procrastinator.

One afternoon, not too long ago, I answered a call from my client, Robert. In November 2010, we had refinanced his $216,000 loan at a fixed, thirty-year rate of 4.375 percent. This had made his monthly payments about $1,078. In the interim, he had heard rates had dropped to 3.5 percent. So, he wanted to know if it would be feasible to refinance and, if so, how much it would cost. He also let me know he wanted to fix the property's bathroom, which would cost an additional $10,000.

"Anything else?" I asked.

"It would be excellent to pay off my children's student loans," he replied.

"What would be the total amount you would like to add to the loan?" I asked.

"About $60,000," he said.

I quickly calculated the numbers and said, "Okay. If you have a new loan of $265,000 at 3.5 percent, with closing costs of about $1,600, your new payments are going to be about $1,189. Alternatively, you *could have 3.625 percent and no closing costs, which would take you to monthly payments of around $1,208. That's around $18 higher. Given the closing costs of $1,600, it could take you seven years to break even. For an extra $110 per month, you could accomplish many objectives."*

Luckily, Robert had all the Five Cs, so he qualified beautifully. Interest rates had dropped, but in order to guarantee them we needed to lock in the rate immediately. Such a lock can occur only when clients provide all the proper documentation.

After we finished our conversation and I was ready to send him the necessary forms, Robert added, "First, I have to discuss it with my wife."

"Of course," I said, and we both laughed.

We received Robert and his wife's signed documents a week later. Luckily, the rate did not change in the meantime and we were able to lock it in at 3.625 percent.

Any refinancing process requires a broker to put together a huge file that includes all of the potential borrower's necessary documentation. This process actually encourages borrowers to keep their papers in order, too. To ease borrowers' anxiety, we keep much of their information in our records. Nevertheless, most of the documents are only valid for two months and usually need to be updated.

If the refinancing process is delayed for any reason, the documents will need to be renewed. Sometimes we have to wait until the desired interest rate, or at least one that is feasible, shows up. This might take only a few hours or a day, while other times it might take much longer. Either way, we have to be ready and able to provide this information to our clients at all times. At our company, we always strive to refinance all of our clients and put them in an even better position. When a client lacks one of the Cs, we get creative and try to help him or her benefit from the current low rates, which Federal Reserve Chairman Ben Bernanke has promised to keep in place until 2014.

Recently, one of my clients told me she wanted to pay off her loan in ten years. We could have amortized the loan over ten years, but her payments would have been too high. Instead, she chose fifteen years and decided to use her extra money, whenever she has it, to pay down the loan. She wants to pay it down in less than fifteen years.

Another one of my clients, who had been paying his mortgage for seven years, did not want to start all over again with a new loan. A simple calculation showed him that if he took a thirty-year loan but continued to make the same (higher) payments he had been making on his seven-year loan, he would pay off the thirty-year loan in seventeen years. In other words, he would pay down the loan six years earlier than he would have if he had chosen to pay the lower monthly amounts that came with the thirty-year loan.

In general, the longer the loan is, the lower the payments are.

Many potential buyers or refinance customers do not have capacity, one of the Five Cs, because they have lost their jobs or are self-employed and do not report enough income. Yet these are people who, throughout the years, have paid their debts, including mortgage costs, on time every single month. Credit cards have contributed to the shortcomings of many potential borrowers—people who either rang up too much debt or made a few late payments— and even a small credit-related problem is enough to prevent a lender from granting a loan. Capital becomes an issue for some people too.

Lenders like to see reserves, but since so many people are being laid off, reserves are few and far between.

My client Bob was looking to refinance. Fortunately, I was able to find a loan that would drop his payments by $500 a month. There was only one problem. A lender required proof of reserves for a jumbo loan, which is what we needed, and Bob had recently spent a lot of money on remodeling his house. In Bob's case, the proof of reserves amounted to eighteen months of his new monthly payments plus tax insurance: about $90,000.

Bob had money, but it was abroad. He had to bring it to the United States to show where it came from, and only then could the money be counted. Before this could happen, the loan window closed. In this case, the property had plenty of equity, and the borrower had plenty of income and a high credit score. However, the character of the loan required something that he couldn't provide at that time: the capital. Luckily, we found another lender who required only six months of reserves (about $35,000), which was feasible for Bob.

In 2012, when I was working on this book, interest rates were the lowest they had been since the 1950s. We were very busy refinancing mortgages, even though the press was reporting that many borrowers could not be qualified, which was partially true. Of course, those folks who lacked one of the Five Cs could not obtain a new mortgage. The major issue was a lack of collateral, since many properties' values were lower than the loan amounts. In other words, they were "underwater."

HARP 2

In early 2012, a number of important events related to the mortgage business took place. First, in his State of the Union address, President Barack Obama announced his plan to revive the American economy. This plan, which involved his expanding refinancing program, was intended to broaden the administration's previously introduced Home Affordable Refinance Program (HARP) to include privately held mortgages.

When the first phase of HARP, HARP 1, was announced in February 2009, it was expected to help four to five million borrowers with mortgages that reached as high as 125 percent of property value. The loans were worth more than the properties themselves, and people were defaulting left and right. Fannie Mae and Freddie Mac, government-owned enterprises, held these extensive mortgages, and now banks were arranging HARP mortgages. When I first read about HARP, the program reminded me of Albert Einstein's famous definition of insanity: doing the same thing over and over while expecting different results.

Many thousands of the people who applied for those programs were borrowers who had received their mortgages in "good times" **but were not qualified according to the Five Cs.** It did not surprise me that many people defaulted on their HARP loans, later, just as they had on their original loans. The same behavior produced the same results. Thus, only a small percentage of borrowers benefited from HARP 1.

In October 2011, the government decided to remove the 125 percent barrier and allow investment property loans to be included. With the introduction of HARP 2, this became a reality.

When I was a teenager in Riga, we had a scarcity of consumer goods. People had to stand in long lines if something special appeared in the stores. One day, I saw a sports jacket I liked. I told my mom about it. She said to talk to my dad about it and that he would buy it for me. She added, "When Papa gives, take." When I returned to the store, the jackets were sold out. I still like sports jackets, but I no longer need Papa to buy me one. I prefer to do it myself.

I remembered this story when I decided to try my luck at refinancing one of our properties in Las Vegas. This property's amount of "underwater" mortgage was higher than its value by about $100,000, but the interest rate was a steep 6.75 percent, so any reduction would help. For me, as a mortgage professional, the fact that the government was offering HARP 2 didn't make any sense, since I had no collateral (our first C). However, I figured, why not join the crowd?

*It turned out to be not so simple. To be eligible for a HARP 2 loan, your original loan has to be **securitized**: in other words, the loan must have originated or closed before June 1, 2009. It also has to be owned by Fannie Mae or Freddie Mac (check the agencies' websites or call your bank to find this information). Some lenders and programs impose limitations on income and LTV.*

There are other differences in underwriting guidance, too, which can be very confusing, not only between Fannie Mae and Freddie Mac but also between banks. My mortgage was originally executed by Bank of America and then sold to another bank. I called that bank in February. After the bank confirmed my loan was eligible for HARP 2, I was told to call back in April because the bank was not yet set up to process such loans. In April, after leaving several messages, I finally reached someone who told me to call back in May.

In May, I was told I could refinance my loan. The closing costs would be between $4,000 and $5,000, and I would save $85 on monthly payments. Every HARP 2 program requires an escrow account (in this case, an account in which taxes and property insurance are prorated monthly and added to the mortgage payments). None of this excited me. So, I asked the bank when my five-year fixed rate would change to an adjustable rate. "September," I was told, and the rate would be close to 4 percent without my having to do anything. Toward the end of this past July, I received a letter from my new bank. My interest rate was going to drop from 6.75 percent to 3.375 percent. Hurray for adjustable loans!

Does HARP 2 work for others? Yes, we do these loans all the time, but like anything else, they are not for everyone, and it takes expertise to know which lender can help a borrower.

T E N

CONCLUSION

WHAT NEEDS TO BE DONE TO CREATE CHANGE?

Of the Five Cs of underwriting guidelines, capacity is perhaps the most important for our economy at large. The reason is obvious. A person cannot obtain a mortgage if he has no ability to pay for it. Therefore, the solution should seem clear. Instead of spending money and energy on delaying foreclosures, why not find a way to create and *protect* jobs, or find a way to help people *keep* their jobs? This would eliminate foreclosures and many other societal ills. Of course, creating and protecting jobs is easier said than done. The question is, how? I found my answer in the great novel by Garth Stein, *The Art of Racing in the Rain*. The book's narrator is a dog by the name of Enzo. The dog's owner, Denny, is a racecar driver. During the book, Enzo recalls his owner's life philosophy over and over again, which is, "Your car goes where your eyes go."

During the twenty-seven years of our company's existence, we have faced many challenges. During the last three years, we have been able to survive and pay all ten of our employees' salaries, thanks to a line of credit from a local bank. The chairman of the bank recently said the bank has plenty of money to lend, but the difficult part of the equation is finding individuals or businesses willing to take the money.

We had a children's train in one of the local community parks in Riga. When I was fourteen years old, I worked there as a conductor during the summer. I did not get paid for my work. The only compensation I received was the ability to ride the adult train for free. I had to get up early in the morning to go "to work."

My late father always encouraged me. "Never be afraid to work, and you always will find it," he used to tell me. And his words were true. I was always able to find work, regardless of the circumstances or the countries I lived in. I am blessed to have been in the mortgage business for twenty-nine years and the owner of my company for twenty-seven years. I have never been afraid to work and never afraid to work hard, even when I was working for free train rides.

HOW OUR GOVERNMENT "HELPS" US FIND SOLUTIONS

Recent settlements between the attorney general and five major banks totaled $26 billion. This money will go toward helping people in the throes of foreclosure, but it will not help much. It does more to punish banks than it helps people. It is too little, too late. As a result of the settlement, up to $1,500 can go to each person who lost a home and whose life has been shattered, as long as he or she can prove it by filling out several documents and standing in line to beg for money from "banks that are too big to fail."

What the press did not report when covering these settlements was that Bank of America, one of the five banks in the settlement, decided to exit the mortgage banking business by pulling out lines of credit upon which mortgage banks were depending. Other big players followed. Only one year prior to that, MetLife Mortgage had **committed $250 million to support the mortgage broker community**. But then, MetLife had followed Bank of America and abandoned the brokers. All of these organizations cited the same reasons for leaving: government regulations and demands made it impossible to conduct the wholesale mortgage business.

In recent years, the government's focus on the regulation of the mortgage industry is evident. In April 2011, for example, the government imposed limits on how mortgage brokers can be compensated. Prior to this, there was the Secure and Fair Enforcement for Mortgage License Act (SAFE), the National Mortgage Licensing System and Registry (NMLS), the Wall Street Reform and Consumer Finance Protection Act of 2010, and the so-called Dodd/Frank Act. Now, lenders are anticipating changes to a new GFE. Just two years ago, new changes were introduced and lenders are still struggling to understand all the rules. Now mortgage banks have to hire several people to understand how to follow the new Financial Consumer Protection Bureau guidelines that are supposed to "protect" the borrowers.

We live in a reality in which politicians, attorneys, and regulators who know little about the mortgage industry (or about running a business, for that matter) dictate how we should live our lives and generate income to support our families. They introduce fear to keep mortgage professionals in line. In fact, the NMLS registry is full of $10,000 penalties for violations of rules.

I was born and raised in Latvia when it was a communist country. I also lived in Israel, which was created and developed on the basis of socialist idealism. Now, Israel is a capitalist country and has a very strong economy. In the late 1970s, I worked in Greece and was amazed by the huge demonstrations in Athens demanding social justice for all. I remember thinking, "Do they know what they're asking for?" We can all see the condition Greece is in now. When socialist East Germany unified with capitalist West Germany, it took the former East Germans years to get over their dependency on the state. We all know too well what happens when the federal government tries to control the economy. The only thing government control produces is bureaucrats.

This scenario is reminiscent of the story of the frog and the scorpion. The scorpion asks the frog to take him across the river. As the frog is swimming across the river with the scorpion on his back, the scorpion stings the frog. While they are both sinking, the frog exclaims, "But why?"
"Because it is my nature," the scorpion says, as they both drown.

The only type of mortgage that a government-controlled enterprise can produce is a conforming loan. The American people were never "conformed." They never will be.

In nature, a forest fire is a regular event. When an old tree grows big and heavy, it sticks out above the forest. The other trees complain and suffer in its shade until lightning strikes one day, and the resulting fire burns down all of the trees. Then, remarkably, the ashes become fertilizer for the seedlings covered by the decaying trees. A new, young forest comes to life.

AS I WROTE BEFORE, WHERE THERE IS A WILL THERE IS A WAY, AS LONG AS PEOPLE ARE MOTIVATED

The end of last year brought us relief. Like many people in the mortgage origination business, I was grateful for the low interest rates created by the Federal Reserve. The Fed's hope was that lowering mortgage payments would free up some cash for people who would then spend that cash and stimulate the economy; however, this is not a long-term solution. In spite of the low rates, the real-estate industry is sporadic and cyclical. People are afraid that before it gets better it is going to get worse.

It seems appropriate here to repeat a concept I introduced early in this book. Potential homeowners need a mortgage the way a potential picture hanger needs a drill and a nail. The mortgage is just a means to an end. What that picture hanger really needs is a picture hanging on her wall. What those people really need is a house. The drill and the mortgage are the tools we use to meet those goals. The mortgage system in our country should propel us to prosperity. We just have to decide, collectively, that our current government-imposed mortgage system is not acceptable. Could we have a mortgage without the Five Cs? Yes. This depends on the compensating factors.

Let's compare this idea to a chair. A good chair has four legs, or four Cs, and the seat is the fifth C. If you varnish the wood from time to time and replace the cushion, the chair will serve you for a long time. Three-legged stools are flimsy and not completely stable. They are only used in temporary situations, but they serve their purpose. Two-legged chairs are only used for very specified purposes. Plus, with only two legs, those legs had better be exceptionally sturdy. A one-legged piece of furniture is usually a table, although it can be a chair, like a stump in the forest.

In spite of limitations, we still find solutions. The secret is to know the rules of the game: the mortgage game.

Now, I want to share my final story.

Once there was a man who would wake up every night, afraid that there was a monster under his bed. He could not sleep, so he decided to seek professional help. He found a doctor who specialized in this kind of problem. During the first visit, the doctor assured him that he would be cured within six months if he came in twice a week and paid $150 per visit. The man was desperate, so he agreed.

Yet the man did not show up for his first appointment. So, the doctor called him to ask why.

"You will not believe what happened when I left your office," the man said. "I met a friend who asked me why I went to see you. When I told my friend about the monster, he told me to cut the legs off of my bed. So I did. Now I have no problem sleeping."

As most reasonable people know, there are no real monsters under our beds. We only imagine them. So, stop being afraid. The American Dream, like many other good dreams, is very much alive. Make it part of your life. I have made it a part of mine. Let me help you make it a part of yours.

Acknowledgements

I would like to thank my publishing team at Advantage Media Group: Mike Austin, Denis Boyles, Brooke White, Kim Hall, Amy Ropp, Megan Elger, Alison Morse, and Mike Eberly.

Special thanks to my daughter, Tamar Kagan, for editing this book and making it easy to read. And one last big thank you to my assistant, Samantha Regala, who connected all the dots.

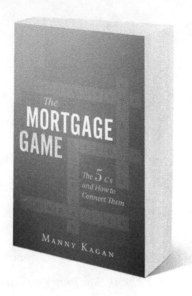

How can you use this book?

MOTIVATE

EDUCATE

THANK

INSPIRE

PROMOTE

CONNECT

Why have a custom version of *The Mortgage Game*?

- Build personal bonds with customers, prospects, employees, donors, and key constituencies
- Develop a long-lasting reminder of your event, milestone, or celebration
- Provide a keepsake that inspires change in behavior and change in lives
- Deliver the ultimate "thank you" gift that remains on coffee tables and bookshelves
- Generate the "wow" factor

Books are thoughtful gifts that provide a genuine sentiment that other promotional items cannot express. They promote employee discussions and interaction, reinforce an event's meaning or location, and they make a lasting impression. Use your book to say "Thank You" and show people that you care.

The Mortgage Game is available in bulk quantities and in customized versions at special discounts for corporate, institutional, and educational purposes. To learn more please contact our Special Sales team at:

1.866.775.1696 • sales@advantageww.com • www.AdvantageSpecialSales.com

Printed in the USA
CPSIA information can be obtained
at www.ICGtesting.com
JSHW012055140824
68134JS00035B/3449

9 781599 323237